The Good
Sex Diet

The Good
Sex Diet

How to Use Food to Transform Your Sex-Life

Arabella Melville

Thorsons
An Imprint of HarperCollins*Publishers*

Thorsons
An Imprint of HarperCollins*Publishers*
77 – 85 Fulham Palace Road,
Hammersmith, London W6 8JB

Published by Thorsons 1991

1   3   5   7   9   10   8   6   4   2

A CIP catalogue record for this book is available
from the British Library.

ISBN 0-7225-2485-4

Typeset by Harper Phototypesetters Limited,
Northampton, England
Printed in Great Britain by
Mackays of Chatham, Kent

To Colin, with love.

Contents

Acknowledgements

Many people have contributed, directly or indirectly, to this book, and I appreciate their help. A few deserve special mention: particularly my partner Colin, who went far beyond the call of duty in co-operating with research. I am grateful to him for reading the first draft of the book and contributing his comments and impressions. Heartfelt thanks also to Charleen Agostini, whose work in helping me through some of my emotional tangles was crucial, and to Pearl Court for her help. Finally, I'd like to thank my dear friend Mike Unger, and John Hardaker of Thorsons, for their suggestions and encouragement.

Introduction:
The Sensual Lover

*I*magine you are eating the most sensuous meal. Across the table, your lover's eyes lock onto yours. You melt inwardly, ravenous with desire, longing to touch. Eating together, knowing you will shortly be making love, you are stretched on the rack of barely-endurable excitement as your passion intensifies.

The blend of delicious food and desire create a delightful synergy of the senses. The scents and flavours of the dishes you share affect your minds and bodies as you tune into your basic animal nature. Eating and sex, both fundamental drives, can potentiate each other, stirring emotions to the boiling point. Lust, nurtured as you eat together, grows to produce skin taut with longing, heightened senses, flushed and sensitive membranes, swollen organs that can only be calmed by the most exquisite contact.

The deepest sexual pleasure blossoms from anticipation. The meal is like a subtle form of foreplay, preparing both body and mind for a greater intensity of experience. When lovers dine together, the digestive juices are not the only ones to flow, for the situation induces delay yet maintains contact. As one appetite is satisfied, another can grow.

The lovers' meal can create an aphrodisiac situation in its own right. But what you eat in that meal is important; food can stimulate or calm your passion. Get the food right and you will enjoy extra benefits that could take your lovemaking beyond the limits of your previous experience.

There's no deception or trickery necessary. In the history and mythology of aphrodisiacs, the rake would slip Spanish Fly or some esoteric love-potion into the glass of the lady he would seduce; he hopes she will become senseless with desire and fall into his arms. In the real world, such potions do not exist. If she did become senseless, it is unlikely to be with desire! And many would-be lovers have been disappointed, some of their victims cruelly poisoned. But the right food shared in the right environment can create conditions that make sex marvellous; while the wrong meal in the wrong circumstances can turn you both off.

You can eat to maintain yourself at the height of your sexual potential, ready to make the most of every opportunity, to taste the best that life can offer. Or you can turn yourself off by eating in such a way that your whole body, your internal and hormonal environment, is just not primed for sex. Intense experiences happen when we are ready for them; as Pasteur said in a very different context, 'Chance favours the prepared mind.'

Food gives us the energy for sex. The right diet keeps our bodies in the healthy balance that Nature interprets as the ideal state for reproduction: eager and fertile. If we want to have babies, building up to this ideal nutritional state is especially important; but even for those of us who may have no intention of reproducing, the same state of physical readiness is most enjoyable. We all want to feel great, full of energy, open to pleasure.

Eating and sex have been linked for as long as human records exist. Sharing food is part of sexual foreplay in every culture. Lovers meet for dinner or romantic lunches; couples eat together before they romp. 'Here with a Loaf of Bread beneath the Bough/A Flask of Wine, a Book of Verse – and Thou . . .'(*Rubaiyat of Omar Khayyam*, translated by Edward Fitzgerald, Collins, 1974.)

I can recall many meals that have acted as preludes for sex: simple and sophisticated, premeditated and unplanned. Usually, it's just been my lover and me; even in a crowded restaurant we are effectively alone: other diners fade into non-existence when my attention is totally devoted to my own partner. But sometimes I've been in a group; sitting opposite a man and watching him, I've felt the longing grow, a longing that draws us away from other people, into our own secret space where passions smoulder, to burst into flame when we are finally and deliciously alone.

I fell for Bill Levy, then editor of the sex magazine *Suck*, over dinner in a Amsterdam. Though surrounded by friends, we had eyes only for each other. His hand brushed against mine at the table, sending an electric current tingling through my body. After the meal we danced, moving our bodies in anticipation of what was to come.

Today it is no longer possible to share our bodies as freely as we thought we could way back then in the sexy 70s, before the dark cloud of AIDS came over the horizon. Today's sexual relationships have a longer, slower development. Courtship is enjoying a resurgence. Casual sex is passé; relationships must last. So understanding how to maintain a sex-life that's as passionate – and even more satisfying – after decades as it was in the first weeks, is crucial for happiness. We need to know how to fan the ardour, how to sustain our love, how to prevent boredom and complacency. We can use all the tricks in the book – but first we have to discover them.

The study of sexual response, and the substances which promote it, is a very old one. Modern science has yet to catch up with all the discoveries of the ancient world, though with every investigation it conducts, more evidence for the validity of traditional knowledge accumulates. Aphrodisiacs have been sought as fervently as the Philosopher's Stone, and for much longer. Every culture uses them, though we in the mundane Western world may be less conscious of the methods we use – and therefore less effective in our use of them – than some earlier, more erotic civilizations.

The familiar cliché, 'the way to a man's heart is through his stomach,' has more meaning than I ever imagined! Aphrodisiacs take many forms. Some stimulate the senses or the whole body, heightening awareness of our sexuality. Others provide nutrients that are essential for peak sexual function. Yet others work by suggestion, reminding us of sexual smells, tastes, textures, sensations. And others again release us from the strait-jacket of puritan inhibitions, allowing us to experience the delights that Nature provides, but nurture may suppress.

Some aphrodisiacs are drugs, acting directly to change the state of our bodies or minds. I shall not explore most of this area because drugs that can have these effects tend to be either illegal or available on prescription only, and all drugs are potentially harmful. However, this book would be incomplete without a discussion of one of the most widely used social drugs of the Western world: alcohol. It is the subject of Chapter 11.

Sexy meals, meals that can turn you and your partner on to the most delightful excesses, are more than a cocktail of drugs and nutrients, however carefully thought out. Aphrodisiac meals are examples of erotic creativity, where imagination combines with understanding to bring out the sensuality of those who share the food. And sharing is the key; there's no magic potion that can make your beloved fall for you against his or her will; no aphrodisiac philtre will generate passion in another person unless the chemistry between the two of you is right. But given co-operation with a partner who could see you as a potential lover, you can harness the powers that nature provides to excite another person and stimulate thoughts of sexual delights.

When the mind is ready, the body responds. Here, too, the clever cook can enhance the capacity for pleasure with which Nature so generously endows us, so that you can enjoy each other for as long as you like, with an intensity of feeling that will remain with you when the body is replete, the appetites totally sated.

Sex is about continued life: about immortality. The power of our sexual drive comes from the genetic imperative that's programmed into every one of us before we are born. But even sex can get boring if you let it, in spite of the fact that it's such a basic drive. We need to explore our potential, to discover new ways of expressing and developing our sexuality, to open new and unexpected doors of experience.

Food, too, is about life: food and sex are the two great drives that direct our activities. The two are linked at many levels. Boring food isn't sexy. Sexy food is about pleasure and laughter and deep satisfying sensuality all at the same time.

Sharing adds to the delight of both food and sex. We can get much higher together. Sharing food can be transformed into sexual foreplay, foreplay that works at a mental and sensual level. It works when we create the right atmosphere, thinking sexy thoughts as we share our food, talking up our feelings, choosing food that's conducive to a sexy atmosphere in an environment that enhances closeness.

That atmosphere is something we create with our minds. Each of us is responsible for our own state of sexual eagerness; it can be all too easy to imagine that your partner has to be a great lover in order to produce your responsiveness. That's a cop-out that will undermine your happiness; great lovers come in pairs. And anyone can be a partner in that sort of excellence; if you play your part with enthusiasm, your lover will rise to the challenge – or the bait.

Thinking good thoughts is the first part of the turn-on. When you tune into your desires, you begin to transmit the messages that create the response you want in your partner. Communication happens on many levels. Preparing food or setting up the meal that you'll share can be the first step towards achieving your own satisfaction. One couple I know finds it difficult to get past this stage – they get so turned on by the interaction as they slowly prepare food together that they often have to take a siesta together before they eat! Through their movements around the close confines of the warm kitchen, through suggestive actions and conversation, they rouse each other to undeniable fever-pitch.

The drive starts in your own mind and permeates your body so that you automatically produce the signals that turn your lover on. All you have to do is relax, let the experience build and the messages flow. Describe your feelings, your desires. Tune into the process of arousal; you can deliberately strengthen the signals so that your lover responds with the passion that brings pleasure to you both.

Sex binds couples together. It is curious that long-term fidelity seems to be becoming increasingly rare when we imagine we understand so much about sex. Perhaps part of the reason for the perilous state of so many relationships is that we neglect the arts of love and courtship. We tend to focus too readily on the genital aspects of sex, forgetting the mental turn-on, the slow build-up of passion.

We need to sustain the joy of our relationships, re-creating the delights of courtship time and time again, through decades of closeness. We can't afford to let fidelity get dull, so that we seek our pleasures outside long-term relationships, imagining that intense sensations require the novelty of new partners. That way lies unhappiness. Today we need to use the arts of love and seduction not just to create but to maintain erotic partnerships.

As we get older, the physical turn-on grows slower and perhaps less demanding. But when the body no longer drives us in search of procreative opportunity, the mind can still energize the body to seek the pleasures that keep us vital and potent right into old age. While our interest in sex is sustained, life itself keeps its colour, its excitement, its value.

Eating right will help to maintain your sexual potential throughout your life. Constantly renewing the delight of our physical and emotional lives means creating new sensations, new pleasures; seeking more intense experiences, exploring deeper into our sensuality.

The Good Sex Diet is about both aspects of the connection between food and sex: about choosing food that can intensify sexual pleasure in the short term, and about the sort of diet that will enhance and sustain your sexiness in the long term. And the recipes dotted throughout this book are designed to make all your juices flow more freely.

In this book, I shall be sharing knowledge and experience that keep my partner and me content, year after year. I can truthfully say that we enjoy greater harmony and more mind-blowing excitement now, after seventeen years of living, working and loving together, than we did in the first flush of our love.

Introduction

Researching this book proved an unexpected bonus to us both; when I was asked if I would write it, I felt at first reluctant; but what I've discovered has brought enhanced pleasure to our relationship. One of the great things about sex is that even if you think you know a lot about it, there's always more to learn! I have gathered together a potent mixture of ancient knowledge of food and love, mingled with the findings of modern scientific research into the way our minds and bodies respond. My sexiest friends have freely contributed their secrets; I shall not risk embarrassing them by acknowledging most of them by their real names, but they will recognize themselves in these pages, and I thank them.

—1—
Aphrodisia and
Ambrosia

*A*phrodite – or Venus, as the Romans called her – was the bringer of joy. The Goddess of love and sex, she could charm everyone, mortal or immortal, human or animal. Her smile was radiant. If she brought trouble and pain it was never her intention; unfortunately others, jealous of her loveliness or resenting her easy promiscuity, would sometimes punish those who fell under her spell. Paris awarded her the golden apple as the most beautiful of the Goddesses; his reward was Helen of Troy, but he lost land and power when he put love before ambition (the Goddess Hera) and war (Athena). Under the influence of Aphrodite, people's hearts fill with the frenzy of desire so potent that they can betray families and leave everything to follow love.

It was Aphrodite who rose naked from the sea-foam, transformed from the severed genitals of Uranus after his castration by his son Cronus. Carried on a seashell, she landed on Cyprus, where one of her many temples was built. She had many children. One was Eros (Cupid), who brought harmony where there had been chaos and created mischief with his arrows which stirred the fires of passion. Another of her children was Priapus, he of the oversized genitals; a third, Hermaphrodite, both male and female. Aphrodite protected marriage but prostitutes too were sacred to her. Sexual pleasure was what mattered; the social context tended to get neglected.

It is entirely apt that this Goddess' name should be given to substances that enhance the pleasure of sexual activity. Aphrodisiacs were very popular in the ancient world. In Rome they were much used to restore the sexual powers of jaded nobility. But their use was not without problems; it is said that the Emperor Caligula was quite a reasonable man before his wife fed him aphrodisiac philtres of such dangerous potency that he became mad. Many supposedly aphrodisiac brews were poisonous; eventually the Emperor Vespasian issued a decree that whoever supplied an aphrodisiac that proved fatal should be fined and exiled or executed!

Poisoning people was far from the sort of activity that Aphrodite indulged in. Her domain was pleasure, not pain. But aphrodisiacs have a grim history. In Victorian times, when trade in aphrodisiacs flourished behind the hypocrisy of strict public morals, several cases of malicious poisoning were brought to court. Even today, laws remain on the statute books to protect British people from unwanted administration of supposedly aphrodisiac substances. Under the Sexual Offences Act of 1956, 'It is an offence for a person to apply, or administer to, or cause to be taken by a woman, any drug, matter or thing with intent to stupefy or overpower her so as thereby to enable any man to have unlawful sexual intercourse with her.'

As recently as this century, women have been poisoned by Spanish Fly, one of the most notorious of supposed aphrodisiacs. There was a case in the 1930s of two women who died after eating coconut ice laced with Spanish Fly; a frustrated clerk imagined that this awful substance would make them fall over themselves with uncontrollable desire for him. Sadly, it did nothing of the sort; the women suffered horribly before their deaths.

The death toll continues today, though it is animals who suffer more than people. The African rhino has been virtually hunted to extinction because its horn is believed by many throughout the world to be a potent aphrodisiac. It is still included in some Chinese medicines, and conservationists are very concerned that rhinos are even now being killed to meet the demand, despite their protected status. In South Africa, Cape fur seals have been slaughtered by the thousand because their testicles are imagined to have aphrodisiac properties. Protests from animal welfare and conservation groups led to a temporary halt in the killing, but the Taiwanese businessman who organized the slaughter has been given permission to kill nearly 6,000 more bull seals.

The sad truth is that all these unpleasant aphrodisiacs, far from creating the life-giving joy bestowed by the Goddess, are either useless or dangerous. Cynical exploitation is not the way to aphrodisia. Rhino horn and animal testicles are incapable of conferring any benefit except to the intact animal on whom they grow.

Spanish Fly, made from the dried and crushed bodies of beetles, is frankly poisonous. Its reputation as an aphrodisiac developed because it damages the urethra, the tube that passes through the penis, causing persistent and painful erections. It does not enhance sexual pleasure, desire, or ability. Aphrodite loved animals, and those who truly seek to follow her would refuse exploitation and cruelty in the false name of aphrodisia.

Ambrosia – food of the gods – would be much more to her taste. And there are many delicious foods that do have genuine aphrodisiac qualities. Lists of foods and other substances reputed to be aphrodisiacs run to great lengths and include substances that are common as well as many that are not readily available. The range is enormous, from herbs such as basil to obscure plant extracts like Fo-Ti-Tieng. Some are stimulants, such as yohimbine, made from the bark of an African tree, which is obtainable in some parts of the world (including the United States, but not Britain); others are pharmaceutical products which have been observed, on occasion, to produce renewed sexual activity in hospitalized patients.

It is very difficult to *prove* that any substance acts as an aphrodisiac. Scientists have attempted to measure the effects of drugs on the sexual behaviour of laboratory animals, but, as you can imagine, such tests are crude at best, and they are at any rate unlikely to produce any useful information about subtle effects on humans.

There have for example been experiments where scientists administer drugs and measure the time taken before a male rat caged with a female will attempt intercourse; they have measured the length of time he takes to initiate sexual contact and the frequency with which the sex act is repeated. Some drugs – one particularly nasty one called PCPA (parachlorophenylalanine) comes to mind – have such dramatic effects that these crude measures do indeed demonstrate changes in sex drive. PCPA undoubtedly acts as an aphrodisiac in rats. It also makes them insomniac, aggressive, hypersensitive to pain, kills their appetites and makes them thoroughly miserable. I know because when I was doing research in psychopharmacology, my rats were injected with PCPA. The effects are appalling. I wouldn't give it to my worst enemy.

Most aphrodisiacs would fail tests like these. The changes they produce are too subtle to measure in coarse laboratory experiments. But you can't say that because a herb or spice doesn't reduce the time it takes the male rat to become interested in sex, it won't affect the human male who takes it in the course of a sexually-charged luncheon with the woman he desires.

Neither can science *disprove* anything: nobody can truthfully say that because an experiment shows no effect, there is no effect. It may be the method of measurement, or the situation, that is at fault. Sexual desire between humans is a subtle thing. If you put me in a laboratory, I very much doubt that I'd feel frisky, whatever drug or food you gave me. The clinical environment is just not conducive to love – as sperm donors often discover.

It is therefore tremendously difficult to be sure whether something is an aphrodisiac or not. In the absence of any clear indication, all you can do is try it out. In the interests of research, my partner and I have been testing the effects on ourselves of the aphrodisiacs in this book; and we've had great fun doing it! Remember too that if you *believe* an aphrodisiac will work, you're already much of the way towards ensuring that you'll get the effects you want. Sexual energy is very suggestible.

Ginseng is one of the best-known and best-researched of the aphrodisiac herbs. It is said that only Siberian ginseng has this special quality; other types are less potent. Certainly ginseng can act as a stimulant and enhance stamina; the Russians have carried out many tests and are sufficiently convinced to administer it regularly to their athletes to enhance their performance. What ginseng does for their sexual performance is not, to my knowledge, recorded. But my experience is that athletes make powerful and exciting lovers – with or without ginseng! And the better the athlete, the more energy and stamina he or she has for sex when not in training.

Personally, I never noticed any effect on my sexual feeling when I took ginseng, nor did those of my friends who used it observe any obvious benefit of this sort. That's not to say there was no aphrodisiac effect; but these things are subtle, and the effects of ginseng are not immediate. Try it if you like: it is not dangerous, it can be helpful, and it is made from plants, not threatened species of animals.

Like ginseng, catuaba is a plant product which is said to enhance sexual drive and pleasure. Catuaba is prepared from the bark of a tree from the Amazon rain-forest; it can be made into tea or swallowed in capsule form. It has a longstanding reputation, particularly for reviving the sexual potency of older people. Whether this reputation is justified is a question that only research at the University of Rio may answer; all I can truthfully say is that it seems to do no harm, and it may well be beneficial.

Another rain-forest herb, the fruit of the guarana tree, is a stimulant which can give you more energy with which to enjoy your sexuality. Guarana definitely does work – without producing irritability or a hangover. We find that a couple of capsules can enliven us when we're feeling tired, enhancing our creativity and generally bringing greater *joie de vivre*. The effect is much more marked than that of ginseng, but there's been less research into it so we know nothing about possible long-term effects. The Amazonian rain-forest is a potential source of many valuable products – which is just one of the many reasons for doing all we can to protect it.

A variety of spices are said to have aphrodisiac qualities; indeed, the Puritans banned the use of spices, which, they claimed, 'excite the passions'. Nutmeg, ginger, cayenne pepper, saffron and cinnamon are good examples. Chapter 10 will tell you more.

Aphrodisiac properties tend to get ascribed to exotic foods. When potatoes were new and rare, they were used as aphrodisiacs. The literature of the period reflects this: for example, a play of 1618 (*The Loyal Subject* by John Fletcher), contains the lines: 'Will your lordship please to taste a fine potato? 'Twill advance your withered state, fill your honour with noble itches.' In Shakespeare's *Merry Wives of Windsor*, Falstaff says 'Let the sky rain potatoes!' Disguised with a buck's head, he's obviously thinking about sex: 'Send me a cool rut-time, Jove,' he implores; then, 'Who comes here? My doe?' Seeing the lady he's after, he greets her as 'My doe with the black scut' and calls on the heavens to shower them with aphrodisiacs, from kissing comfits (spiced sweets) to potatoes – 'Let there come a tempest of provocation.'

But when potatoes became common, their reputation was lost. Similarly, tomatoes – once known as love-apples – were thought to stimulate passion, until Victorian times, when almost everybody was eating them. It was probably the redness of tomatoes that conferred their reputation; red is the colour of passion. Anything that is reminiscent in appearance of excited sexual organs was likely to have aphrodisiac qualities attributed to it. While powdered rhino horn – despite the shape of the intact organ – confers no benefit, aphrodisiacs can work because they remind us of sex. It can be any quality of a food: its shape, its smell, its texture, its colour. The Chinese regard peaches as aphrodisiacs because the rounded, rosy-flushed fruit with its silky cleft inspires thoughts of the naked behind of a beautiful girl. Obviously, if peaches were ground into a powder, they wouldn't have the same impact.

The taut purple skin of the aubergine reminds me of dark-skinned lovers, and to my mind the taste of caviar is just like that of sperm. Both have strong reputations as aphrodisiacs. The stinkhorn fungus (*Phallus impudicens*) looks exactly like a cock growing out of the ground, with its mucus-sheened glans-like cap on a five-inch shaft; personally, I wouldn't dream of eating it, though some cultures do – it's too repulsive and smelly to turn me on! I want my aphrodisiacs, like my men, to smell and taste delicious: the earth can keep its fly-blown fungal phallus.

The texture of sex-organs is smooth and silky, and food that has these qualities is well on the way to being aphrodisiac. The flavours, salt and rich, are mimicked by some meat and fish dishes; indeed one talented Cordon Bleu chef said candidly that her secret was to make the food taste of sex. Her appreciative clientele would travel regularly from London to her restaurant in the West Country to savour these cunningly prepared dishes.

There are other realities behind the myths and ancient wisdom in the choice of aphrodisiacs throughout the world. Seafoods, sacred to Aphrodite because of her birth in the sea, contain nutrients that genuinely do sustain sexual function. Oysters, the most famous of the aphrodisiac seafoods, are especially rich in such vitamins and minerals. A remarkably high proportion of foods with reputations as aphrodisiacs contain large quantities of vitamin E, and many contain zinc. The importance of these nutrients will be explained in Chapter 3. Other aphrodisiac foods, including avocado and chocolate, contain substances that act like drugs which are capable of affecting sex-drive.

Foods that contain the power to generate whole new organisms – eggs, nuts and seeds – are included in many lists of aphrodisiacs. As a group, they are very concentrated sources of nutrition. It's doubtful that they stimulate the sex organs or the passions directly, but these concentrated foods do provide the energy and nutrients we need to function at our best without overloading our stomachs. The story of the Negro Mimoun, which is told in that classic work of erotica *The Perfumed Garden*, tells how he accomplished fifty days of copulation with the insatiable Mouna, sustained only on egg-yolks and bread. So delighted were they both with the experience that they were married at the end of it. It wasn't a balanced diet, but it certainly seemed to provide stamina!

Aphrodisiacs can work at many levels, but the effects they have depend on the situation in which they're consumed. Sexuality is complex; it's far more than a simple physiological reflex. Physical sensations can be coloured and experienced in a variety of ways, depending on your mental state.

Anger and excitement, for example, are both states of high arousal mediated by the flow of adrenalin through the body. Psychologists have demonstrated that inducing a physiological state of arousal artificially with injections of adrenalin does not allow them to predict the response that results; that is determined by the situation. If something happens to annoy you when there's a lot of adrenalin flowing through your body, you're liable to get violently angry; but if you're with a comedian, you'll laugh till you cry. Adrenalin makes experience more intense, it doesn't fix its character. So any substance that could work as an aphrodisiac when you're with a favoured lover might just make you irritable if your partner proves boring!

For this reason, feeding any aphrodisiac to unwilling partners will not of itself change their attitude to sex or to you. They may respond in the way you want if you are able to seduce them with honeyed words, charm them with your attentions, or otherwise make yourself so attractive that resistance crumbles. And that doesn't happen unless the person you desire is ready to be tempted by your advances. No drug, no food, no magic philtre, will do the trick otherwise.

There can be no fail-safe aphrodisiac, but there are aphrodisiac situations, aphrodisiac meals – and there most certainly are effective *anaphrodisiacs*, capable of turning you or your partner off or damaging one's ability to perform. Oral contraceptives act as anaphrodisiacs on some women, especially those who grow bloated and depressed when they use them. It's ironic that a contraceptive, designed to make sex safe – even casual – can kill the desire for it!

Some medicines, particularly tranquillizers, diuretics and drugs which reduce blood-pressure, can reduce desire and make men impotent. If you have to take any of these, you should work on changing your lifestyle so that they are no longer necessary. One of my earlier books, *Alternatives to Drugs* (Fontana, 1987; American edition *Health Without Drugs*, Fireside (Simon & Schuster), 1990), explains how to set about improving your health in order to reduce your need for medicine. You will also find that if you follow the advice in the last two chapters of this book assiduously, you will be less likely to need lust-killing drugs.

To sum up, there are some substances, notably alcohol but also the humble potato, that can act as aphrodisiacs if you use them right, but produce the opposite effect if you have too much. It's a matter of fine judgment, one on which later chapters of this book will advise. As a general principle, excess of *anything* is likely to interfere with your sexual pleasure – except, perhaps, for kisses and caresses!

—2—
Licking Our
Lips

*W*hat makes a sexy meal? A candlelit table in a secluded corner of a French restaurant, the air sweet with the perfume of roses, sultry music in the background . . . Watching each other, hot with anticipation; lingering glances, electric touches, low voices rich with desire . . . Or a picnic on a rug in a woodland clearing, birdsong in the air, the sun sparkling on the clear water of a brook, your bodies tingling with closeness . . .

The food seems almost irrelevant! You nibble, you taste, but you're not so much hungry for nourishment as for love.

But the food is important. With the right food, all your senses are sharpened; you respond to both the food and the way it affects you both. You are intensely aware of your lover's movements, tuned into the visual impact of eating, the sensual delight of food intensifying sexual feelings.

We make love with our eyes, responding at a deep level to the way our partner's pupils widen and darken with desire. We gaze at our lover's lips, tongue, teeth: imagining them working on our bodies, nibbling, sucking, licking, kissing. We fantasize about devouring each other in a sexual frenzy. Food becomes a metaphor for the lover's body.

Atmosphere can be important too. Love might grow in a brightly-lit, cluttered kitchen or a tacky café with overflowing ashtrays and sticky table-tops, but then it happens despite the environment. To boost excitement we should create or seek out a situation which fits our mood.

At table, arrange to sit opposite each other, close together, so that you can look into one another's eyes. The eyes are very important to sexual attraction: they signal, more clearly and accurately than anything else, the way we feel. So don't wear sunglasses; don't wear glasses at all if you can avoid it. Emphasizing the eyes with darkened lashes and kohl exaggerates their impact. Eye make-up isn't just vanity, it's a sexual come-on.

You're watching your lover, watching you. Sometimes it becomes too much to bear; you drop your eyes. But not for long if the fascination's strong. Be cautious when your lover won't look straight at you: is he or she nervous, embarrassed, edgy, not really interested? Maybe you don't need to talk much: your eyes, lips and hands talk for you. As you eat, you transmit messages. The tongue caresses food as it would caress your lover's body; if the food suggests the body, so much the better.

Consider, as you eat, the nature of the messages you transmit. I wouldn't want to be insensitively gobbled or slurped up: I like to be consumed delicately – at least at first! And the food should suggest this: choose small and tasty morsels rather than large hunks, food to be savoured and appreciated as you would like to be appreciated.

Some of the sexiest food is inherently suggestive. If possible, pick it up with your fingers: the hands are sexier than cutlery. It doesn't matter if it's sticky; sex is sticky. Sex is smooth, silky, yielding or firm; sex has a heady aroma, a rich flavour. Lick your fingers carefully, don't wipe them: do with your tongue on your own hands what you would do on your lover's body. And savour the flavours as you would the lover that you may shortly taste.

The lips and tongue – red, the colour of passion – are givers of pleasure so exquisite that consciousness itself is clouded by their touch. As you eat, as you watch your lover eating, think about these things. Anticipate and feel your ardour intensifying. Talk about the way you feel: let the heat grow within you, warming your lover.

The meal is part of your foreplay. As your digestive juices flow, so will your sexual juices. Sex is a slow-burning fire that grows hotter and hotter the longer you tend it. Not for me the sudden flare that's over almost before it has warmed me; the sensual lover lets passion build higher.

Like a good meal, sex takes time and imagination. Hurried sex is a waste of energy which gets boring very quickly. I'm talking about the real thing, unforgettable passion, lust that makes you tremble all over.

If you've ever watched animals courting, you'll see how important the pre-coital build-up can be. You may think that because the ram penetrates the ewe only briefly that he is a coarse and insensitive lover. But this is not so. There is an extended period of courtship before sex. He coos gently to her; he tastes and sniffs her until he is sure that she is ready for him; the pair rub their bodies together, look into each other's eyes, lie together, stay close. Observe the pigeons, how they dance together, watching each other, circling around, facing each other until the last moment when their excitement has reached the critical point. Listen to the tom-cat singing to his sweetheart for hours together, see how she rolls and teases before she allows him to come to her.

We humans have the biggest brains, the sexiest natures. We can make love at any time; for many of us, sexual love is tremendously important to our happiness and our relationships. We should not allow our love-making to deteriorate to a level of sensitivity below that of the other animals. We have the advantage of sophisticated knowledge, the ability to share skills and experience so that the discoveries of a 16th-century Sheik and 20th-century psychologists are equally available to us. We can be the greatest experts in the arts of love.

All this requires thought and careful arrangement. For while we are such sexy beings, we are also highly temperamental, emotional, susceptible to a host of anxieties and turn-offs. We need to ensure that everything is conducive to joy, so that we may fully experience all that we are capable of.

The food may contain aphrodisiacs, but that is only part of the story. It is the whole situation that can create erotic appeal. It's the way you dress (of course) – in colours that delight the eye, shapes that emphasize the contours and movement of your body, textures that ask to be stroked. It's the way you smell when you lean close, the perfume of your hair and body. Natural perfumes like fresh sweat can be sexy; I appreciate a man who smells of exercise, but you have to judge this sort of turn-on very carefully.

We all produce aphrodisiac scents, called *pheromones*, particularly from our hairy parts – our armpits and around our sex organs; this hair exists to collect and concentrate the smell. But it goes sour all too easily, and if you're nervous, you might secrete the wrong odours altogether! The smell of fear isn't sexy. So think positive, think randy, think about the sort of encounter you've been looking forward to; dismiss ideas that it could all go embarrassingly wrong.

Adding perfume can supplement the exciting smell of pheromones; quality perfumes often contain substances like musk, which can add to your sex-appeal. Washing all your natural scent away with deodorant soap is a mistake. For women, soaping the genital area, spraying it with deodorants or using antiseptic douches is an even greater mistake; these products not only wash away the special perfumes, called *copulins*, that turn men on, but they upset the delicate biological balance of the vulva, increasing susceptibility to infection (and its associated nasty smells). Use warm water, with a little salt and vinegar added if you wish; but nothing more.

The perfume of your food should complement the perfume of your body. Choose flavours for their sex-appeal; the recipes in this book offer my selection, but you'll doubtless think of your own when you focus your mind on romance.

Sharing food can be very sexy. Dipping into the same pot, fingers touching, eyes meeting – you are enhancing the closeness. Try feeding your partner with tasty morsels as birds do. I recall a handsome cockerel who used to live in our garden; he lived there along with our three hens. If he found something really delicious to eat, he would not hog it for himself; instead, he would call his ladies over and offer them the delicacy.

You and I might not get turned on by the offer of a small frog, but those hens got very excited! The time my partner gave the cockerel a piece of fresh cream doughnut is a very special memory. The cockerel tasted it, found it delightful, and crowed excitedly, calling the hens to join him. Then he stood back proudly, the perfect gentleman, as they divided the morsel between them. No sooner had they finished than he leapt on the back of the closest hen.

Now, I'm not suggesting that we should follow the chickens' example too closely; the hens got very fed up with the cockerel's insistent sexual demands, and for all his occasional gallantry, he wasn't much of a gentleman most of the time. But that way he had of giving his partners the very best was a habit from which we can learn.

It's charming to be offered the most delicious morsels from one's partner's plate, to be fed the tastiest pieces of food by your lover. Concerns about hygiene and ladylike behaviour should be forgotten: sex is about intimate sharing, and you shouldn't hesitate to eat from your partner's fork or take food from his or her fingers.

In some ways, sexual interaction can be a reflection of the intimacy that we had with our mothers: nothing is hidden, generosity and love are total. So it can be when, as adults, we love each other. Feeding each other is an expression of feeling. Nurturing each other, on every level, is a way of demonstrating love. So when you pop a grape into your lover's mouth, or proffer a forkful of meat from your own plate to your lover's lips, you are making symbolic gestures that emphasize your closeness.

As you eat with your lover, remember that the way you eat can be seductive. Imagine eating an ice-cream cone in the most suggestive way possible: curling your tongue up the sides of the ice-cream, tickling its tip, taking the whole thing into your mouth . . .'this is what I will do to *you*', you say with your eyes; 'think how my tongue will feel on your most intimate parts.' Look straight at your lover as you do it. The message will come over just as clearly as you want. And the clearer it is in your own mind, the greater the response you'll get.

I have been told that the idle movement of my fingers stroking up and down a tall glass can stop the conversation in a whole bar. I'm sure that's an exaggeration, but there is a nucleus of truth in it. Opportunities arise frequently during the course of a meal for suggestive actions, for touches and movements that remind your partner of what you'd like to be doing together. George Bernard Shaw described dancing as the vertical expression of a horizontal desire; we can dance subtly with our hands, revealing our desire through a whole variety of actions. Develop your erotic consciousness: not self-consciousness, which is isolating and divisive, but consciousness of the erotic projection of the self.

Talking about sex keeps the mind on the subject, primes the body for action. The most erotic table-talk concerns your experience of love, your anticipation and desires. Use it with care, and only when you want to follow on to the bedroom – I've been caught out in the past, casually chatting about my sex-life without realizing that the man opposite me at the table was getting very turned on! Now I'm older, I'm not so naïve that I imagine such conversation to be neutral; I know it can have a strong impact.

Of course, you also have to be sensitive about explicit sex talk. It could be too much for a shy lover. And it's distinctly unpleasant for someone who doesn't fancy you to be subjected to your erotic tales – this is not a ploy for overcoming reluctance, it's far too steamy. Don't talk about other people who have sexy features that your companion doesn't share: don't describe another lady's luscious bosom to a small-breasted woman, or the pleasure you had with a particularly well-endowed man when your companion might be insecure about the size of his own equipment. Comparing one's mediocre self with an unknown but exciting other is a quick way to eliminate confidence and a total turn-off. Don't let careless words lead your partner down this stony track.

Whatever else you talk about, never mar the pleasure of a sexy meal with discussion of mundane topics like money, illness, or problems at work. Keep off depressing issues like pollution and the state of the world. Create a warm cocoon around yourselves; this is not the time to look at worrying developments outside. Nothing turns off sexual ardour faster than anxiety.

For a slow turn-off, there are few things more effective than television. If you're watching TV, how can you concentrate on your lover? When TV is more interesting than the interaction between you, you're not tuned into sex. Can you imagine the goggling couple, TV dinners on their laps, turning away from the box and towards each other? They're thinking about the soap, or the Middle East, or Patrick Moore's tailor, even when the programme is about heavenly bodies. So telly addicts, switch off! Because if you don't, your partner surely will.

Music is a different matter entirely. Music can enhance sexual pleasure at every stage. 'If music be the food of love, play on!' said the bard. What music is suitable is a personal matter; you might prefer Madonna or Hendrix, Vivaldi or Chopin. The special thing about music is that it can seep into our subconscious, enhancing the rhythms of our bodies. Sometimes it's blatantly sexy. The Doors were obsessed with sex. Sex and drugs and rock 'n roll . . .the sexual revolution of the 1960s had a persistent beat behind it.

Finally, you need warmth and comfort. Heat (short of the enervating, oppressive kind) stimulates desire. As you peel off layers of clothing, exposing your body, you make yourself more available and more attractive. Warm perfume in the air – whether the natural scent of honeysuckle or night-scented stock, smoke from perfumed wood or burning incense – heightens the passions. Your dining room should be free from draughts, furnished with soft fabrics, rounded shapes and rich colours. Shiny steel and sharp angles have no sensuality about them; these are the forms of a technological culture that values cold money over warm human contact, the synthetic over the natural. To enjoy sex to its full, we must be in tune with nature – our nature.

It's this ability to tune into Nature and the intense urges that are natural to us that can make a picnic into such a sexy affair. Think of Manet's famous painting *Dejeuner sur l'Herbe*. Painted in 1863, this Impressionist masterpiece scandalized traditional classicists with its overt sensuality: a group of people, including a naked woman in a sensuous pose, eat together as they soak up the sun. In a secluded glade amid tall trees, the picnickers become part of the riot of growth and reproduction that is the natural world. There are few things more delightful than making love in the open air; what a pity there are so many people that privacy outdoors is such a rarity!

One of the sexiest picnics I ever had was on a hot summer's day in North Wales. After negotiating a long, rocky path over a remote coastal headland, my friend Jerry and I unpacked a simple lunch of bread, cheese and fruit and settled down to share it on a sun-baked rock facing the sea. Afterwards, relaxed and replete, we began making love slowly to the sound of the waves below us. We did not fear intruders: we had seen nobody for hours, we were in a very isolated place. Only the sheep would find us here. We threw inhibition to the winds, kissing and pleasuring each other's naked body as the fancy took us.

It was not until our passion was spent that we looked around to observe an astonishing number of small boats. All seemed to have engine trouble, or had stopped to fish, or for some other reason were stationary just out to sea. But by that time we were too content to care about the spectacle they must have witnessed. I hope they enjoyed it – We certainly had!

—3—
A Potent

Combination

*E*ating for sexual pleasure has two aspects. There's the traditional view of the aphrodisiac as a food that packs an instant wallop, followed, you hope, by the Big Bang; and there's the Steady State of sexual readiness, punctured by periodic supernovae and black holes.

But physiology diverges from cosmology. The steady state must come first; you aren't likely to enjoy that Big Bang as much as you might unless your body is prepared for it. A good-sex diet incorporates both aspects; it will enhance your capacity for sex by getting your body into a state of optimum health, and it shows you how you can use food to help create the special highs that you will then be capable of experiencing. Through eating right, you can achieve that potent combination of general preparedness and powerful aphrodisia that can make sex really special.

It is true that you are what you eat. When you follow the guidelines of the good sex diet, your body will not only be healthier and more attractive, but more prepared for sex. You will smell sweeter and taste better. You might achieve a good sex-life despite a poor diet, but your enhanced pleasure in sex and ready desire when you eat right could surprise you.

The good sex diet is a way of eating that will keep you energetic and fully alive, so that your body is able to respond to the aphrodisiacs that I'll be describing in later chapters. Those exquisite moments of ecstasy require an underlying readiness, because this is what determines the way your body and mind functions, which in turn affects the way you respond to sexual stimulation.

Many aphrodisiac foods, as I shall explain, contain nutrients that can improve sexual ability, but good nutritional status develops over a long period of time. The sexiest people are neither too fat nor too thin; their hormone levels are correctly balanced; they have vitality, stamina and energy. All these depend on the right sort of diet.

Your everyday diet should meet all the needs of your body and mind. It should provide plenty of energy, keep your heart and circulatory system working well, prevent uncontrolled swings of hormones, and keep you as lean as you want to be without suffering the debilitating effects of calorie-controlled dieting.

If you care about your body, you won't want to mistreat it – or not regularly anyway! Life and health are precious, and good sex is an expression of the joy of being alive. Eating right is part of the way you keep that life-force flowing strongly, maintaining the energy that fires your sexual furnace.

Our food needs vary from day to day with the changing demands of our lives and the fluctuations of our hormone systems. Sometimes the need for particular nutrients is very high; the good sex diet will build up your reserves of these nutrients so that your ability to enjoy life will be enhanced.

This is particularly true for women, whose bodies and minds fluctuate with the monthly cycles of female sex hormones; many women suffer from deficiencies in the nutrients that are necessary to keep them stable and productive in the face of this constant change. Loss of sexual interest among women is often linked with shortage of essential nutrients.

Young people, brim-full of life-energy, may be able to get away with eating haphazardly, without care, and still find their sexual energy stays high. But we're not all like that – I never was – and as we get older, we can't expect to rely on these in-built energies: they don't stay with us indefinitely without the right replenishment.

A diet that keeps you in tip-top sexual form will also maintain your general health. Healthy people are naturally sexier. They look sexier; their skin glows, their hair is glossy, their flesh firm, they have a spring in their step; they feel stronger and more confident; they enjoy their bodies and the energy that good health confers. But for most people, health isn't an accident of fate, it's the product of the right lifestyle.

Eating for health means being careful to select the types of food you need, making positive choices about diet so that you know you're getting everything you should have. Treat your body right today so that it serves you well tomorrow, next year, and a decade hence.

If you know that the things you particularly love are not good for you, you should save these special foods for special occasions when you can enjoy them without anxiety. Some of the ingredients of the recipes in this book are just the sort of luxuries that would be damaging if we ate them too often. But keeping them as treats means delicious foods stay special, never becoming dull or mundane. Your celebrations will be all the more exciting when you decide to have them.

The next few chapters are about specific foods with aphrodisiac reputations. Some of these you might well eat every day, but others – such as chocolate and champagne – will lose their effectiveness and reduce your capacity for sexual pleasure if you have too much of them. Fruit, vegetables, nuts and seafood are good sources of nutrients that you need on a daily basis, but exotic foods may lose their magic if you have them often.

Sex, like food, gets boring when it's always the same. The level of excitement varies from time to time, according to mood, circumstance, and the amount of preparation and energy you're willing to put into it. If you scale the peaks of pleasure at the weekend, you'll need a few days to recover, both emotionally and physically. If you try to make every night more exciting than the last, moving rapidly from high to high, you'll find you get jaded, always seeking more extreme, intense experiences in the hope of re-kindling fires that have burned themselves out.

Casanova is reputed to have consumed fifty oysters for breakfast, day in, day out. Oysters to him must have become as unexciting as porridge may be to you and me: a good start to the day, but not the sort of thing that inspires you to leap into bed in a sexual frenzy! Nevertheless, all those oysters probably stood him in good stead, providing high levels of the nutrients that are crucial to sexiness. But no aphrodisiac, however nutritious, is sufficient to reverse the effects of long-term poor eating habits.

Meeting our natural appetites is always enjoyable: Nature created us that way. It's the distortion of our culture that brings in feelings like fear, shame, and guilt. We have to get totally away from such negative ways of thinking. Instead, we need to retain our desires, nurturing our sense of pleasure by remaining in touch with our inner selves. Ignoring your needs in one area of life can damage your ability to enjoy its other aspects. Depriving yourself of good food will slowly destroy your sexual appetite.

So the good sex diet is a positive, joyful way of eating designed to ensure that you get what you want and what you need without doing yourself harm.

The first rule is that you should never wilfully deprive yourself of good food: eat whenever you're hungry. Don't worry if you're eating a lot; especially don't worry if you're consuming what you believe are too many calories. Calories have nothing to do with the nutritional value of food; even as a measure of its energy value they are inadequate, because they ignore the nutrients you need to use that energy. For our metabolic processes to work as they should, we need a whole range of micro-nutrients, and some high-calorie foods are especially rich in the nutrients essential for energy production.

To stay sexy and healthy, we need energy. Energy makes life exciting. Food is the source of that energy, and you need enough of it to keep yourself on top form. Deprive yourself of nutritious food, and you will quickly find that you can't produce energy you want when you want it. You'll tire easily, you'll have little stamina – you'll lose your *joie de vivre*. Go for nutritional value even if it sometimes comes with a lot of calories. Later in this chapter I'll explain in more detail what I mean by nutritious, quality food.

Eating properly is one way of telling yourself that you matter. You feed your body well because you value it. Truly sexy people are in tune with their bodies and their desires, and they look after themselves. To celebrate the best of which you are capable, you have to appreciate yourself, care for yourself, treat yourself with love. And that includes feeding yourself properly and making sure your body's needs are met. Learn to trust and act upon the messages that you get from your body about your needs. We can get quite clear messages about the food we should eat, and when we should eat it; research has shown that even young children will select a balanced diet when they are given a wide choice of foods. So heed your desires and follow your appetites – have confidence in your self!

If you've been living on junk food or distorting your perception by dieting, you may need to train yourself to interpret those inner signals correctly. When you next feel like eating, ask yourself what it is you really need to eat – don't just grab whatever's to hand, or what you habitually have. Tune into your desires and try to meet them with the simplest, most natural food you can. Think about the way you feel as you eat: is this food meeting your needs? Or is it not quite right? Try something different if you're doubtful. But try to avoid processed food, for that will confuse your delicately balanced appetite systems.

Some people find it difficult to choose the right sort of food. Their selections are heavily influenced by what's convenient or most often available in shops and cafés. So they eat to suit the priorities of the food industry, not their own personal needs. It can be difficult to break free of these cultural pressures, but you will feel healthier and sexier when you do.

The problem arises because food today is not the same as the food we evolved to eat; it has been altered and distorted by the food industry. Most of the food in supermarkets and cafés is processed, the goodness removed so that the final product has a longer shelf-life or more 'added value'; salt, sugar, flavour-enhancers, colours and additives are put in to increase your desire to eat the denatured products of food manufacturers; fats are altered chemically and stabilized to create substances that keep well on the supermarket shelves but do you little good.

The flabby bodies of the people who live on convenience foods are just not sexy! Watch them at supermarket checkouts; see what their trolleys contain. It's a terrible warning for all who are willing to heed it! If you want to look and feel as good as you possibly can, you can't afford to leave your choice of diet to chance and convenience. Food is far too important for that.

If you eat processed foods regularly, you lose touch with your needs because your taste buds were not designed to make sense of the balance of chemicals in them. We learn to seek excessively sweet or salty things not because we will benefit from eating them, but because we have become accustomed to them. To train yourself to know what you need, you have to return to the sorts of foods that are closer to their natural state. Natural foods, with all the goodness left in them, are much better for you.

Always choose food for its nutritional value. You don't need to be an expert to do this; all natural wholefoods include valuable nutrients in addition to whatever protein, energy or fat they may contain. Wholefoods are usually brown rather than white; they include whole-meal bread, whole grains like brown rice, and whole vegetables.

Wholefoods should form the bulk of your diet. They contain more vitamins and minerals, as well as fibre to keep your digestive system healthy. Processed foods and 'junk food' don't contain enough of the micro-nutrients you need to derive the energy you want from them, so you are more likely to turn them into fat. When you try to get energy from things like sugar and other highly-refined foods, your nutritional status actually declines as your body takes nutrients from store to cope with nutrient-deficient calories. As time goes on, your access to energy diminishes. Obviously this is bad for your sex life.

The best food of all is fresh organic food. Organic food contains higher levels of micro-nutrients than food produced by chemical farming methods, because organic farmers replace everything that comes out of the soil with natural balanced fertilizers, whereas conventional farmers just pile in three chemicals – nitrogen, phosphate and potassium. These chemicals actually interfere with the plant's ability to take up important minerals from the soil. So the crops produced by conventional farming are inevitably deficient in the varied minerals you need for a good sex life.

If the only change you make in your diet is from refined food to organic wholefood, your health will benefit and you will have more energy to enjoy life and sex. You'll start to shed excess weight and your skin and hair will improve. The difference in the nutrient content of the two types of food really is that significant!

You may imagine that wholefoods – all those lentils and brown rice – are tasteless. This is a myth. If you experiment, you'll find it all depends on preparation. An unskilled cook can always produce flavourless food; but when you take care with cooking, you will find that wholefood meals have richer, more varied flavours than you can ever achieve with refined stuff. It may be that the wholefood meals you've had have been prepared with much less seasoning than you're used to; and of course they don't contain the synthetic flavour-enhancers with which you may have been fooling your taste buds. In fact, surveys prove that organic wholefoods have much more flavour than conventional equivalents.

To be sure of getting all the micro-nutrients you need, go for a varied diet. Include a wide range of unprocessed grains, vegetables, nuts and fruits; these alone are sufficient to keep you well nourished. If you're not vegetarian or vegan, you'll also enjoy fish, meat, eggs and dairy produce; but your health will be better if you have relatively little of these rich protein foods each day. Three or four ounces – one portion a day – is quite sufficient for most people.

Except on special occasions, avoid sugar in all its forms. White sugar is so refined that it can be regarded as a pure chemical; brown sugar isn't much better. Do not be taken in by advertising that suggests that sugars like glucose and fructose are significantly better; you don't need these either, except in their natural form in fruit and vegetables.

Avoid all refined foods, everything made of white flour and

everything from which the goodness has been removed, such as white rice and white spaghetti. Also avoid food that contains added fat, such as biscuits, pastry and chips. These foods can make you fat without providing the nutrients that make you feel good. Women who regularly eat foods containing processed fats, or repeatedly heated fats such as the oil used to fry chips, are particularly likely to suffer from problems with their sex hormone balance. Natural fats, particularly in nuts and seeds, are beneficial; processed fats are not.

Regrettably, no fats are as wholesome as they used to be, because dangerous artificial chemicals called organochlorines have entered the food chains. These poisons are concentrated in animal fats and fish oils and include PCBs, dioxins, pesticides, wood preservers, dry-cleaning fluids and industrial solvents; dumped into rivers, the sea and in landfills, and sprayed on the ground and onto crops, they pollute the water, evaporate and fall in the rain.

In the oceans organochlorines are concentrated by plankton. Little fish eat plankton; big fish eat little fish; we eat big fish . . . and at each step the concentration of organochlorines increases. On the land, organochlorines in pasture and crops are concentrated in grazing animals. This phenomenon, called bio-magnification, means that carnivores and omnivores like ourselves get the largest dose.

Organochlorines damage the immune system, concentrate in the ovaries and testes, causing sterility, and pollute body fat, crossing the placenta during pregnancy to harm the developing baby. When our bodies attempt to de-toxify organochlorines, the enzymes produced to break them down can be ineffective and their power directed against hormones and other essential components of our bodies. Thus these chemicals cause multi-faceted damage which can affect our ability to function sexually and in every other way.

We cannot completely avoid organochlorines but we can minimize our exposure to them by avoiding animal fats and fish oils, and choosing vegetable oils instead.

I'm not going to give details of precisely what you should eat each day, because such rules don't work. We are all different, our needs individual. Some people thrive on a diet that's almost entirely carbohydrate – grains, vegetables, fruit. Others find they need more fat and protein to feel satisfied, and they will tend to go for more animal foods. Neither type is more or less sexy than the other, so long as each person's needs are effectively met; it's a question of discovering the type of diet that suits you as an individual, tuning into the way you feel when you eat one way or another. I've known some very sexy carnivorous people and some equally sexy vegetarians.

For years there used to be a sandwich-board man who would stand on Oxford Street in London proclaiming that protein inflames the passions. His message was that we should all give up eating meat because it makes us randy. I often wondered how many people took his message to heart and *increased* their meat consumption! But the truth is that you can be as randy as a rabbit on rabbit-food – if that's what suits you personally.

Diana is one of the sexiest ladies I've ever met. She now lives with a successful rock musician, but when I knew her she used to make blue films for fun, and very good they were too. You could watch her perform in films that were explicit but still charming, without the falseness that usually renders such films sleazy and unconvincing.

A lithe, slender person, Diana had so much sexual energy she'd happily share her bed with two or three friends; nobody was left out. She was also very fit and an accomplished dancer. But she was a strict vegan, eating no animal foods at all. She got all the nourishment she needed from nuts, beans, grains and vegetables: food that provides a range of nutrients adequate for good health and good sex.

Research has shown clearly that vegetarians and vegans are, in general, healthier and slimmer than meat-eaters. However, we are all different. The sort of diet that kept Diana in top form in every sense just doesn't seem adequate to everyone; you may discover you just don't feel right unless you have some meat or fish.

I believe that because of the way humans evolved, men are more likely to feel they need animal foods than women. Male and female hormone patterns are different, and our bodies are made up differently. Men should have more muscle and less fat; their bodies are tuned to produce explosive power, while women can continue for longer at a lower power output. We have different fuelling systems, and different organ weights within our bodies.

Women are nibblers. They should eat smaller, more frequent meals with a higher vegetable content. This is because our ancestresses were gatherers, collecting roots, fruits and nuts from the environment around them, while the men would go off on hunting expeditions with periods of fasting before capturing the animals they brought back as meat for the tribe. Then they would feast to celebrate success in the hunt.

Women are also relatively more sensitive to pollutants in food, and so should minimize their consumption of butter, cheese, full-fat milk and fatty meats, especially those that come from animals reared in intensive conditions, such as pork and bacon. Make a fresh cream cake or dessert really count by indulging consciously, when you're deliberately titillating your senses with your lover.

The right hormone balance is crucial both for a high level of sexual interest and to maximize your ability to enjoy sexual activity. This is especially true for women, who have to ensure that they're getting the right nutrients lest they risk losing that sense of joy in living for a large part of the month when their hormone balance goes awry. Three-quarters of women suffer from pre-menstrual problems which can undermine their sexual responsiveness; for them, eating plenty of fresh food of vegetable origin – especially seeds and nuts – is most important. My book, *Natural Hormone Health* (Thorsons, 1990), explains in detail how diet influences female hormones.

The importance of nutrients to improve hormone balance and enhance sexual responsiveness was brought home to me by Jane, a reporter who had had a hysterectomy while still in her forties. After her operation Jane lost interest in sex; while her desire for closeness remained, she didn't get aroused and she ceased to be capable of having orgasms. But when she changed her diet so that she got more of the essential nutrients she needed, and added multi-vitamin and multi-mineral supplements to make up the shortfall she suspected she suffered, she discovered to her delight that her capacity for sexual pleasure returned.

The micro-nutrients that are known to be particularly important to keep both women and men functioning sexually include the B-group vitamins, vitamins C and E, the minerals magnesium, iron, zinc and boron, and essential fatty acids. If your diet has been poor or you have digestive problems such as food allergies that reduce your absorption of micro-nutrients, you may benefit from supplements that include these nutrients.

But taking supplements won't make up for the hazards of a poor diet; if you use them at all, they should be in addition to plenty of nutritious food. Normally, the body absorbs nutrients better from food than from supplements, partly because their chemical structure is matched to our needs, and partly because food contains a wide variety of interacting nutrients which are more effective when they're absorbed together.

Vitamin E has been called the sex vitamin because a deficiency of it causes impotence in male animals from rats to men. It is essential for female fertility and it can reduce menopausal symptoms such as hot flushes. If you suspect you would benefit from increasing your vitamin E intake, eat sunflower seeds – they're great for quick snacks when you feel peckish; use cold-pressed sunflower oil, which can be mixed with cider vinegar to make salad dressings; and choose sunflower margarine. Other good sources of vitamin E are almonds, hazelnuts and peanuts, avocados, sweet potatoes and wild blackberries.

Vitamin C is essential for the production of sex hormones. It is concentrated in the adrenal glands, which produce testosterone, the hormone which makes both men and women feel sexy. People with high body testosterone levels have higher sex drives; they tend to be more assertive and less prone to depression. Smoking, infection and exposure to pollution will increase your need for vitamin C.

Get your vitamin C from fresh fruit and vegetables, especially broccoli, watercress and new potatoes; from citrus and berry fruits such as oranges, grapefruit and strawberries; from pineapple, melon and tropical fruits. Make sure you have at least one portion of these vitamin-rich foods every day. Storage and cooking reduce the vitamin C content of food, so the fresher it is, the better.

B-group vitamins are necessary for energy, normal brain function and stable mood; people who are running short of these vitamins feel too miserable and lethargic to be sexy! If you are prone to depression, anxiety or sleeping problems, try increasing your intake of B-group vitamins. They are found in whole grain products such as wholemeal bread and brown rice; wheatgerm is a very rich source and a useful supplement that you can sprinkle on cereals. Vitamin B_6 is particularly important for women; it can reduce both PMT and menopausal distress. Rich sources of B_6 include oily fish, egg-yolk, grains, nuts and seeds, bananas and avocados.

Zinc is probably the most important mineral for the proper development and function of the male sex organs. Boys who grow up on a diet that's zinc-deficient have tiny genital organs; they don't develop into men unless they receive extra zinc. Serious zinc deficiency in adult men causes impotence, while less severe deficiency reduces fertility. Semen is very rich in zinc: a single ejaculation can provide a milligram of zinc – nearly a tenth of your daily requirement! The recipient may benefit, but a man who ejaculates frequently may have to think about replacing the zinc he's giving away.

Zinc is essential for women, too, although they can generally manage with less than men. However, zinc deficiency in either sex will reduce sex drive, cause anxiety, depression and anorexia, and reduce resistance to infection. You're likely to need extra zinc if you're very physically active or if you are fighting an infection, because muscle-building and the immune system demand zinc.

The richest source of zinc, by far, is oysters. Was this the secret of Casanova's sexual appetite? Other zinc-rich foods are red meat, nuts, and organic whole grains.

Magnesium and *iron* are essential for energy and hormone balance. With both of these minerals, the first symptom of deficiency is often a lack of energy; in the case of magnesium the problem develops because you need magnesium to produce energy from food, while iron is essential for production of red blood cells, which carry oxygen to every part of our bodies. When your muscles don't get enough oxygen, you feel drained of energy and lack stamina.

Red meat and green or red vegetables are rich in iron; this is what creates the dark colours in Nature. But people who get plenty of iron in their diets may still be short of it because many of the drinks we have with food can interfere with iron absorption. Tea, coffee and fizzy drinks that contain phosphates can cause this problem; don't have these with your meals. If you change to pure fruit juice to accompany your meals, your iron absorption will be enhanced by the vitamin C it contains.

Boron is a trace mineral whose role in sexual health has only recently been discovered. It is especially important for middle-aged and elderly women because it raises the level of the female sex hormone oestrogen. Older women are prone to oestrogen shortage when their ovaries cease to produce it; if they eat more boron-rich foods, such as fresh fruit and vegetables, their oestrogen levels can double. Oestrogen is necessary to keep the female sexual organs functioning as they should; when it runs low, women can suffer from vaginal soreness and dryness. So every woman who wants to remain sexy into old age should make sure that she gets plenty of boron by eating fruit and vegetables every day.

Finally, we all need *essential fatty acids*. For women, these beneficial fats keep sex hormones in a healthy balance, helping to prevent premenstrual problems, period pain and menopausal miseries. For men they are particularly important to maintain a healthy heart and circulatory system. Sexual activity demands good cardiovascular function; penile erection depends on an adequate blood supply, and we all know how the heartbeat quickens with excitement! So every sexy man should look after his heart by ensuring he gets enough essential fatty acids to keep it working well.

There are two major sources of beneficial fats: oily fish, such as herring, mackerel and salmon; and seeds such as sunflower and pumpkin. For some people, the best sources of essential fatty acid are evening primrose oil and blackcurrant oil; these contain readily absorbed oils, which are good for those whose bodies are not good at transforming beneficial fats into the form which the body needs.

If your diet contains a lot of processed fats or animal fat, you will need more essential fatty acids to balance them. Different types of fat compete in the body, and those who have too much of the wrong types may start to experience a shortage of the forms they need. So getting your essential fatty acid levels up involves not only choosing foods that contain them, but avoiding foods that contain potentially harmful fats. If you eat a lot of biscuits, fried food, full-fat dairy produce such as butter, cheese and cream, or if you go for fatty meat products such as sausages, you will exaggerate any shortfall in essential fatty acids.

Sexy people don't go for fry-ups and big plates of greasy food. Even lumberjacks grow big bellies on that type of diet, and most of us are far less active than they! So watch the fat in your diet; select foods that contain good fats, but cut down on those dangerous processed and animal fats. That way, you'll keep a youthful figure and a healthy heart.

Some people refuse many of the foods recommended here, especially nuts, avocados and grains, because they're seen as fattening. Don't worry about that! Perhaps you think you'll be sexier if you lose weight, and maybe you're right; but you should not try to shed excess pounds by avoiding foods that will help you to enjoy your sexuality more. As I explained earlier, counting calories doesn't work in the long term because it ignores the nutrient content of different foods. Foods like nuts and avocados, which are rich in high-calorie essential fats, are necessary to your body.

Don't imagine that eating as much as you feel you want is a route to greater problems; the truth is that dieting by any of the conventional methods, such as counting calories or giving up carbohydrates or fats, will both make you fat *and* diminish your sex drive!

Being sexy means being in touch with your body and your feelings; not overruling but exploring desires, following them without fear or shame. Like sex, food can be a source of intense anxiety, especially for people who are unhappy with themselves; they feel guilty when they indulge, ashamed of loss of self-control, disgusted with themselves. I know about those feelings: I used to be a dieter, rejecting my body because I saw myself as fat. It's no coincidence that I couldn't enjoy my sexuality at that time either.

It's quite true that excessive fat is rarely considered sexy. It's not healthy either. But the way to free yourself from fat, if that is your problem (and it may not really be so – I wasn't actually fat when I starved myself: I just thought I was) is to eat *more of the right food* – not to continue eating the same junk as you have been, while cutting down on calories.

In particular, make a conscious effort to eat more vegetables every day; have more meals based on vegetables (potatoes are fine!) and help yourself to larger portions. That way, you won't feel tempted by sweet or fatty foods that will add to your problem. At the same time, increase your energy output by building more exercise into your daily life. As Chapter 13 explains, this will make you feel and look sexier as well as helping you to shed unwanted fat.

Cutting calories deprives you of energy and makes your body shed metabolically active lean tissue. Your body responds to food shortage by conserving energy and conserving fat to keep you alive if famine (from which your body is designed to protect you) continues. When you start to eat normally after a diet, you replace those hard-lost pounds of muscle with fat. So the more you diet, the flabbier you become. The way out of this horrible cycle is to give up dieting – for ever. Resolve to eat right so that you have plenty of energy, and use that energy for activity which will build a shapely body. A book I wrote with my partner Colin Johnson, *Eat Yourself Thin* (Michael Joseph, 1990) explains this strategy in detail.

Of course, on those special days when you're titillating your senses and indulging your appetites, you'll ignore all this sensible advice. That's fine! When you've got the background nutrition right, you'll be able to get away with just about anything. Even that luscious, mouth-watering confection, chocolate . . .

—4—
Dark Magic:
Chocolate

*O*f all the foods linked with love, chocolate is perhaps the greatest aphrodisiac. The dark lady of the taste buds, the melting, luscious temptress, chocolate is the gift of lovers and the comfort of the unloved. From chocolate we create dreams, fashion love-hearts and symbols of passion. Naughty but nice is too weak a description: wicked but wonderful is much more fitting!

You guessed. I love chocolate. Most people do. So, I've found, do dogs, rats, sheep and even hedgehogs! I know of nothing with such wide-ranging appeal. You can get almost any creature to eat out of your hand when you offer chocolate, so if you want your lover eating out of your hand – metaphorically speaking – then feed him or her chocolate!

More taboo than any other food, yet so desirable that addiction is commonplace, chocolate is the most sexy stuff. This is partly because of its smooth texture, its unique flavour, its richness and versatility – but there's more to it than that. Chocolate contains a combination of natural psychoactive chemicals that can influence our minds and inflame our feelings. With chocolate you can be childlike or sophisticated, glutton or gourmet. You can be crude, with a chocolate phallus from a sex shop – or tender, smearing warm chocolate fudge icing on your lover's body, to lick off slowly.

Chocolate has held its reputation as an aphrodisiac for the whole of its recorded history. Its name is derived from that of the Aztec Goddess of Love, Xochiquetzal, who brought it to earth for the delight of humans. Prepared from the cocoa bean, the fruit of a native plant of Central America, chocolate has brought pleasure for many centuries. According to legend, Montezuma, Emperor of the Sun, drank 50 cups of chocolate a day as he sported with his harem of 600 women! Among the Aztecs, chocolate was prepared as a bitter beverage, drunk from golden goblets by the Imperial family and served at wedding feasts to give the bride and groom stamina for their night of love.

Montezuma shared chocolate with Hernan Cortes, the Spanish explorer; history does not record whether he also shared his harem! Cortes brought it back to Charles V of Spain, who described it as 'the divine drink that builds up resistance and fights fatigue.' The Spanish Inquisition, ever alert to the sinfulness of sexual stimulation, soon tried to suppress the consumption of chocolate; but despite their fearsome reputation for torture, they were unable to stamp it out. However, for monks and young girls, chocolate was totally banned. The temptation to sin might become too great.

Prohibition against chocolate in Europe worked no better than it did against alcohol in the United States centuries later, although it remained a rare luxury product because, of course, people couldn't brew it themselves from local ingredients. By the 18th century in England, chocolate had become a social drink. At that time of general licentiousness, religious influences were operating in the opposite way. Puritans, worried about the demon alcohol (which was, presumably, seen as an even worse promoter of sexual licence), began to promote chocolate as an alternative. Religious families – the Rowntrees and the Cadburys – made chocolate their business.

It was not until the 19th century that manufacturers developed the processes necessary to create the chocolate confectionery that we know today. This required the removal of fat from the cocoa bean, and the addition of much more sugar than had been formerly used. The chocolate of Montezuma's time had been a bitter drink, but the Victorians, with ready access to sugar from West Indian plantations, created sweets from cocoa. Then chocolate, no longer the preserve of the rich, really took off. But unlike some other foods which lost their aphrodisiac reputations as they became available to the masses, chocolate retained its association with love.

Chocolate continues to be the stuff of folklore. According to mythology, during a drugs raid on a Rolling Stones party the police discovered Mick Jagger with Marianne Faithfull, naked except for a white fur coat or rug. He was totally preoccupied, licking a Mars Bar inserted into her body. While Ms Faithfull admits to the fur coat, she denies the Mars Bar; untrue though the story may be, the chocolate bar fits and the myth persists. Only a chocolate bar would fit this particular niche; a carrot would be too coarse, a stick of rock too hard, an oyster too slippery. The long-running series of advertisements for chocolate flake (or Cadbury's Phallic, as it's known in my household) and chocolate-covered Turkish Delight are blatantly sexy.

What is it about chocolate that has given it such staying power as an aphrodisiac in the face of great cultural changes? Increasingly, scientists believe that the cocoa bean contains chemicals that directly affect the emotional centres of the brain. Like many natural substances, cocoa contains a variety of subtle chemicals. Some of these have yet to be identified; their role and potential range of effects are not known. But certain components have been recognized. One is phenylethylamine, a stimulant that some believe is associated with feelings of love. There's circumstantial evidence to support the argument; for example, phenylethylamine levels are very low in people who suffer from severe depression. People in this state are unable to feel sexual desire, unable to love. Some of us react to depression by reaching for chocolate; it seems to calm anxiety and make us feel better.

Theobromine and caffeine are other stimulants found in chocolate. Tea and coffee also contain these natural drugs, and both are used as pick-me-ups. Their physiological effects can be quite profound; for example, they can help to open up the airways in asthma sufferers and they may cause breast pain and lumps in women. In chocolate, the combination of these various stimulants and other components whose effects are not yet known are likely to be synergistic; they will enhance each other.

The effects of the chemicals in chocolate are exaggerated by its sugar content. Sugar gives an immediate energy boost; it goes straight into the blood-stream, from whence your body can take it to fuel activity and excitement. It affects the brain as well as the body; if you take carbohydrate (and sugar is the fastest-acting form of carbohydrate) without significant quantities of protein, it selectively encourages uptake of the amino acid tryptophan into the brain. Tryptophan produces mental relaxation; it reduces anxiety and promotes sleep, especially in the evening. So by eating chocolate before retiring to bed, you can put that initial burst of energy to good use to fuel your passion, after which you will feel relaxed and sleepy, ready for a restful night, from which eager lovers will awake recharged.

Chocolate can be addictive. Chocoholics feel high when they've been eating it, low as its effects pass. This could be due to the stimulant drugs it contains, for the related substances in tea and coffee are also mildly addictive. Fortunately, such intense reactions are rare. They reflect unusual sensitivity to the drugs in chocolate. Early in the addiction, chocolate probably brought such a sense of contentment that its 'users' wanted to stay with that feeling all the time; but addictions don't work that way. After a while, the addict feeds his addiction to avoid feeling awful. It's no longer a positive, joyful experience. And as for the effects on the waistline – well, they can be disastrous!

Nor is this the only type of disaster you may meet when you share chocolate with your lover. My dear friend Annabel, a statuesque blonde, is dramatically sensitive to the mental effects of chocolate. Once she starts eating it, she can't restrict herself to one or two pieces, she guzzles the lot. Then, a little while later, she turns nasty – so nasty that those who have lived with her have learned that they could not have chocolate anywhere near her. Nowadays she tends to avoid the stuff; but when she's feeling especially irritable, she'll eat it to punish her boyfriend for the impertinence of daring to love her!

Annabel is one of those people to whom you only give chocolate if you're willing to risk having your head bitten off. A perceptive lover discovered that the way to deal with this was to make passionate love with her immediately after sharing that very special chocolate treat. If your lover is anything like Annabel, light the blue touch-paper and retire *immediately* – together! Do not hang about after eating chocolate if you don't want to get burnt. When the timing was just right, Annabel would be feeling so relaxed and content in the warm aftermath of sex that she would doze off before the reaction set in.

Most people can eat chocolate without becoming chocoholics, just as most people can enjoy the occasional drink without becoming alcoholics. There's a whole range of reactions. Some of us are chocolate lovers who delight in chocolate but restrain ourselves from indulging too regularly. Some consume chocolate daily, without thinking; they may be mildly addicted, just as frequent tea- or coffee-drinkers tend to be addicted to the stimulants these beverages contain. Others are overt addicts, eating enormous amounts of chocolate every day, shaping their lives around their need for chocolate. For them, chocolate deprivation causes intense depression.

To keep chocolate joyful, most of us have to restrict the amount we have. Quite apart from the effects of the drugs it contains, its sugar content can be damaging, especially for people whose blood sugar is not very stable. Refined sugar in chocolate causes a surge of insulin in the blood-stream if you don't burn it up quickly in physical activity. This may be followed by a rebound when blood sugar falls drastically, making you feel tired and irritable.

I think chocolate should be regarded as something special, something we savour consciously and use to enhance our moods. So I go for the very best chocolate I can find, tasting like a connoisseur, selecting chocolate treats as an aficionado chooses vintage wines. For me, over-indulgence is a mistake. Excessive chocolate sits heavy in the belly, producing a sickly, soporific effect. A huge box of chocolates may seem like a dramatic gesture, but I'd recommend giving a large bunch of roses with a small but expensive gift of exclusive chocolate instead. My partner has a different view; he prefers excess, of chocolate as of many things in life: 'Give me chocolate overdose every time!' he says – especially now he's discovered its aphrodisiac effects. But he is a more frequent chocolate eater who doesn't suffer from insulin-rebound problems as I do. In the course of time, we get to know ourselves and our reactions; knowing how you respond to chocolate is essential if you're to get the best from it.

Alternatively, you can incorporate chocolate into delightful desserts. In all the forty-odd years of my life, one particular dessert sticks in my mind as the most gorgeous taste experience: a chocolate mousse served in a skiing lodge in the Pyrenees. This small dish contained the most sensuous mixture. Smooth and silky, its texture was perfect, its dark chocolate flavour exquisite.

The first requirement for a really first-rate mousse is top-quality chocolate; this is what creates the flavour. A specialist chocolatier is the ideal source, but few of us have access to one. So you may have to make do with a bar of the best (plain) chocolate you can find. Always read the labels of chocolate bars; look for the highest cocoa content you can get: some brands contain 45 per cent cocoa solids. The recipe for making your own luscious mousse is on page 57. Make it to serve in a single bowl with two spoons, one for your lover and one for yourself; feed each other by candlelight with succulent morsels dropped softly on the tongue. Then retire to the bedroom to savour its aphrodisiac after-effects!

One word of warning about this recipe: because it contains uncooked eggs, it may pose a health hazard for people who are elderly or in poor health. If you're not very careful about the source of your eggs, there may be a risk of salmonella infection. I always use organic eggs because infection is then much less likely than if you use eggs from hens kept intensively. Organic eggs come from hens that live on a natural diet and are free to roam over large areas; so-called free-range eggs are neither as tasty nor as safe.

Chocolate Mousse

Imperial/Metric		American
4 oz/115g	plain/unsweetened chocolate	1 cup
2 fl oz/60ml	rum or brandy	¼ cup
	2 eggs	
2 oz/55g	quark or fromage frais and	4 tbs
3 fl oz/90ml	fresh double/heavy cream	⅓ cup
	or	
5 fl oz/140ml	double/heavy cream	⅔ cup

- Melt the chocolate by warming it in a basin over a pan of boiling water; adding the rum or brandy as you do so. Allow to cool slightly.
- Separate the eggs, then beat the egg-yolks into your chocolate-and-rum/brandy mixture until it thickens.
- At this point you have to decide whether to use part-quark/fromage frais and part-cream or cream on its own; I prefer the lighter dessert you get with quark, but those who like their food really rich can use cream.
- Whichever you decide, first whip the cream on its own, putting aside two large teaspoonsful to use to decorate the dessert when it's ready. If you are using part-quark add it now to the rest of the cream.
- Beat the egg-whites till they're stiff but not dry, and fold them with the cream/quark mix into the chocolate. Make sure you haven't got any undiluted lumps of chocolate left – if they harden, your mousse will be lumpy!
- Pour into serving dishes and chill for two hours.
- When ready to serve, dollop each portion with a bit of the cream you set aside earlier.

If you're eating a dessert as rich as this at the end of a meal, make sure your main course is light or you could feel too weighed down for sexual indulgence! Get freshly-brewed coffee ready to serve at the same time as the mousse: the combination of hot strong coffee and chocolate mousse is really delicious. My partner Colin and I have been eating a lot of chocolate mousse recently as I experimented with variants of this recipe, and we're convinced that it really does work as a powerful aphrodisiac!

All of us have had the sort of nights that leave us most reluctant to rise bright and early in the morning. When Colin and I do get up late, chocolate cake is our favourite afternoon indulgence. If I'm feeling especially loving, I take Colin out to a restaurant where we can get the most delicious chocolate cake. We eat it with whipped cream. When we don't want to go out, I'll bake the cake myself. Chocolate cake is the ideal treat for a lazy afternoon: before your siesta, perhaps? How about indulging your sense of taste with wickedly delicious cake before retiring to explore the delights of your sense of touch? The following two cake recipes (see pages 59 and 60) are slightly different in character, the first being more chocolaty while the second is richer and better for freezing. Both are totally scrumptious!

Gateau au Chocolat

Imperial/Metric		American
8 oz/225g	plain/unsweetened chocolate	2 cups
2 fl oz/60ml	water	¼ cup
	3 eggs	
3 oz/85g	caster/superfine sugar	½ cup
2 oz/55g	fine plain/all-purpose flour	½ cup
5 fl oz/140ml	double/heavy cream	⅔ cup
	morello cherries for decoration	

Again, use the best chocolate you can find for this recipe; blocks of cooking chocolate that you get in supermarkets don't usually have the best flavour.

- Preheat the oven to 350°F/180°C (Gas Mark 4).
- Line an 8-inch cake tin with oiled greaseproof paper.
- Melt a quarter of the chocolate with the water in a basin over a pan of boiling water. Once it has melted set the chocolate aside.
- Put another basin over your boiling water, this time containing the eggs and sugar. Whisk them together until thick, then remove the bowl from the heat and continue whisking till the bowl is cool. Add this mixture to the melted chocolate.
- Sift the flour and fold into the mixture.
- Turn the mixture into your prepared tin and bake for 45 minutes.
- While the cake is cooking, melt the rest of the chocolate in a basin over a pan of hot water. Set aside to cool slightly.
- Whip the cream, then beat the chocolate and cream together.
- When the cake has cooked and cooled, split it and fill it with a layer of the chocolate cream. Spread the rest of the creamy mixture over the top and sides of the cake. Decorate with curls of chocolate and Morello cherries.

Colin, my partner, likes his chocolate cake hot and his cream cold. For this luscious combination you'll want a chocolate fudge cake. The cake freezes well but you shouldn't ice it until it's defrosted.

Hot Chocolate Fudge Cake with Chilled Cream

Imperial/Metric		American
	Cake:	
4 oz/115g	plain/unsweetened chocolate	1 cup
6 oz/170g	butter or soft margarine	⅔ cup
4 oz/115g	caster/superfine sugar	⅔ cup
	3 eggs	
6 oz/170g	self-raising/self-rising flour	1½ cups
4 fl oz/100 ml	strong coffee	½ cup
1 tsp	vanilla essence/extract	1 tsp
	Frosting:	
4 oz/115g	plain/unsweetened chocolate	1 cup
2 tbs	rum	2 tbs
2 oz/55g	butter	¼ cup
4 oz/115g	sifted icing/confectioner's sugar	⅔ cup
	walnuts for decoration	
	When ready to serve:	
5 fl oz/140ml	double/heavy cream, whipped and chilled	⅔ cup

- Preheat the oven to 350°F/180°C (Gas Mark 4).
- Line an 8-inch cake tin with buttered greaseproof paper.
- Warm the chocolate in a basin over a pan of boiling water.
- Beat the butter and sugar together until pale and fluffy and add to the melted chocolate.
- Beat in the eggs one at a time.
- Fold in the flour, coffee and vanilla.

- Turn the mixture into the cake tin and bake for about one hour. Cool in the tin for half an hour before turning out.
- For the frosting, melt the chocolate with the rum over hot water.
- Beat in the butter, allow to cool a little, then beat in the icing sugar.
- Spread this mixture on the cooled cake and decorate with walnuts.
- If you like your cake warm, pop the portion you're about to eat into a microwave and heat for 2 minutes at medium power. Dollop with cream and serve immediately.

The contrasts are what make this an extra-special treat. White cream against dark cake; hot with cold. Sex is an extreme thing; love brings joy and tears in turn, passionate determination and melting submission.

My final chocolate recipe is another combination of contrasts: Pear Marilyn (see page 62).

Pear Marilyn

1 round, ripe dessert pear
chocolate ice-cream to taste
hot chocolate sauce to taste

You can create a very sexy shape from a plump ripe pear.

● Cut the pear in half lengthwise and remove the core. Peel
carefully.
● Thinking of Marilyn Monroe, use a sharp kitchen knife to sculpt
her back, with rounded buttocks (not forgetting the small
dimples either side of the spine) and curved hips.
● If the pear is at all hard, microwave in a closed dish for 5 minutes
with a little sugar and brandy. Leave to cool.
● Lay the pear, buttocks up, on a bed of ice-cream. Pour hot
chocolate sauce around your lovely lady just before serving.

It's possible to buy quite good chocolate sauces, but if you want to
make your own, it's very easy (see page 63).

Chocolate sauce

Imperial/Metric		American
2 oz/55g	plain/unsweetened chocolate	½ cup
1 tbs	milk	1 tbs
1 tsp	vanilla essence/extract	1 tsp

- Melt the chocolate with the milk and vanilla the over a pan of hot water.
- Stir well.
- Serve hot.

If you dream of licking chocolate off of your lover's body, you can use chocolate sauce or fudge icing – but make sure it's warm! Also, beware pouring on so much that you can't cope with eating it all: this can be the messiest form of sex-play.

—5—
Love in a
Sea-Shell

*W*hen Aphrodite rose from the waves to bring love to the world, she embodied the link between sex and the sea. Botticelli's gorgeous goddess is the most familiar image of Aphrodite; long hair modestly held over her pubic area, she stands in all her curvaceous glory on a mammoth cockle-shell, travelling the waves of the Mediterranean.

Mind you, I think she'd seem more sexy to 20th-century eyes if she were portrayed as less coy, her posture more responsive to the sea's motion. Aphrodite wasn't the modest, passive maiden of classical painting; I can easily imagine her surfing on her sea-shell! Surfing is definitely sexy, with its exhilarating plunges into the depths alternating with rapid rises to the peaks of powerful waves. When the wave crashes over the surfer's body, overwhelming him or her in its foaming ecstasy, what could be closer to the perfect metaphor for orgasm?

Sun, sea and sex: as millions of annual devotees know, they go together so well! It's hardly surprising that seafood should have such a long association with love.

Do however be sure to move away from the beach to make love – sand does awful things to delicate membranes! But when you bring the fruits of the sea home with you, you are taking a taste of its sexual magic. Because the sea not only stimulates sexual feelings, it carries the salty flavour of sex and offers the perfect food to nurture our sexual selves.

Every type of food from the sea can contribute to the good sex diet. Perhaps the most exciting and the most beneficial is the oyster, long respected as an aphrodisiac.

In nutritional terms, oysters are special because they're uniquely rich in zinc, a mineral that is crucial to the development of sexual organs and to sexual pleasure. To complement the zinc, they contain vitamin E, which is also essential for sex and fertility.

Zinc-deficient young men become impotent; supplementation, according to micro-nutrient expert Dr Carl C. Pfeiffer, can make 'masturbation or sex . . . more gratifying'. Zinc is essential to the prostate gland and to the formation of normal sperm.

Fertility in both men and women depends on adequate zinc levels. It can help childless couples to conceive, and it's essential during pregnancy for the birth of a healthy baby. So if your sex-life is disappointing, perhaps you should take a tip from Casanova and eat a dozen oysters a day!

It's not their nutrient content that makes oysters so exciting, however; it's their appearance – and above all, their texture.

People have strong opinions about raw oysters; they either love them or they hate them. Some of my friends adore them; others – the majority – detest them. Colin's view is that he'd rather suck a sheet of corrugated iron if he wants zinc! Nevertheless, I can see why many people think they're the most naturally erotic things you could ever hope to eat.

Raw oysters are served on their shells, the smooth mollusc set against glowing mother-of-pearl. In appearance an oyster is reminiscent of a vulva; to the tongue it feels very sexy indeed. There's nothing as smooth as a raw oyster. 'They slide down your throat like kisses,' my friend Rosie explained, 'It's the way they feel in the mouth that's so erotic.'

If only oysters were pink and warm! Cold, greyish oysters strike me as having necrophiliac appeal – definitely not to my taste. But, I have to admit, I'm prejudiced. I tried oysters washed down with champagne, in the company of a man I've loved dearly for many years – yet even so I had difficulty finishing my half-dozen. If I weren't so sincerely dedicated to research, I would have left them – I thought they were quite disgusting. And no, I didn't end up feeling unexpectedly randy!

What I did feel was that eating oysters definitely shares some common sensations with fellatio. I remind myself that some people find oral sex disgusting – perhaps they react to their lovers the way I react to oysters? I'm told oysters are an acquired taste; perhaps oral sex is, too.

Despite their reputation as aphrodisiacs, I don't recommend that you dash out and buy a dozen oysters as a treat for your lover unless you have firm reason to believe he or she will enjoy them! If you want to experiment and you both retain your sense of humour, you might have fun trying them together. You might even adore them.

But if your lover reacts like my friend Anne, eating oysters won't bring you closer! Her view – which I share, to some degree – is that when eating a raw oyster 'the challenge is to keep from heaving when it hits your stomach.' Anne thinks the passion for oysters is all hyperbole; in her opinion, eating raw oysters is 'a rite of passage into high society that's about as exciting as initiation rituals at school.'

Yet oyster bars are very popular, especially in France, the land of gourmets. The French adoration of oysters has a long history; they've been gathered off the shores of Brittany since Roman times. Louis XV commissioned for one of the dining rooms at Versailles a massive painting of *Le Déjeuner d'Huitres* (The Oyster Dinner); it portrays the aristocratic court enjoying a feast.

Napoleon, in common with successive kings of France, adored oysters; no doubt Josephine reaped the benefits. But the French consumed so many that the natural oyster beds of Brittany were seriously depleted, and a decree was passed by Napoleon III that limited the numbers that could be taken. Since then, native oyster beds throughout Europe have been protected, and oyster fishing is banned during the molluscs' summer breeding season.

The two main species of oyster are the native oysters, or *huitres plat*, and rock oysters, also known as Pacific oysters or *creuses*. Native oysters, highly prized for their flavour, are only sold between August 4 and May 15. If you want to taste them at their very best, try them in mid- to late October, or at the end of the season (April to May). The more prolific, if less tasty, Pacific oyster is available all the year round. European oysters cost three times as much as the crinkly-shelled Pacific oysters.

From Belgium I heard a tale akin to Casanova's legendary love of oysters. Christopher, an oyster entrepreneur, told me of a day he was sitting in a Brussels bar, chatting with the proprietor, whom he knew well. Two ladies came and joined him and they fell into conversation over plates of oysters. When the ladies left, the barman began to giggle. 'What's the joke?', Christopher wanted to know. It emerged that these ladies were prostitutes, preparing for work that afternoon. Every day, before going out to meet their clients, they would consume two or three dozen oysters each. As he pointed out, their earnings must have been substantial for them to be able to afford such a diet; so perhaps oysters made them particularly good at their work!

Oysters should be served in the lower half of their shells, on a bed of cracked ice and lettuce, accompanied by brown bread and butter. Get them from the best fishmonger you know; if you're in any doubt about how to prepare them, get them opened and cleaned before you take them home. Or, of course, go to an oyster restaurant such as Wheeler's in London or The Oyster Bar in New York!

Before eating the oysters, squeeze lemon juice over them; sprinkle on black pepper and Tabasco sauce if you like it. Loosen each oyster so that it slides sensuously off the shell and into your mouth. Some people swallow oysters whole, others prefer to chew them. Their flavour is very delicate.

Oysters are traditionally served with champagne, and are associated with parties and festivities: 'La magie de la fête et des nuits Parisiennes,' enthused one French author; 'There is always a sort of mysterious pleasure, a stylish celebration in sharing a dinner or a supper of oysters. They breathe an atmosphere of gallant parties, at once precious and simple, like the oyster herself, fruit of the sea and the work of men.' (*L'Huitre, son Histoire, sa Culture* by Jacques Frugier, Retour des Parcs, 1988)

Even if raw oysters don't appeal to you, you may love them cooked. Try them rolled in beaten egg and breadcrumbs, then quickly fried in butter. Served piping hot, they lose their clamminess and turn into delightful morsels.

Although oysters have a unique reputation as aphrodisiacs, other types of seafood are perfect for sexy dinners. Low in harmful fats but high in protein and other nutrients, food from the sea is very conducive to a joyful sex-life. It sits light on the stomach, giving you energy and enhancing health.

Lobsters can make the perfect dinner dish for lovers. Eat them sensuously, using your hands to pick the pink and white flesh from the rosy shell, sucking on the claws as you'd kiss your lover's fingers. To my mind, however, preparing and cooking your own lobster is too much trouble; it's definitely a restaurant dish!

Fish roe, too, has a well-deserved aphrodisiac reputation. At the top of the culinary scale comes caviar, the black eggs of the sturgeon which was reputed to have sustained that randy Russian Empress, Catherine the Great. Eggs of all sorts carry new life, which is what sex is all about. But caviar tastes sexy too.

My first thought on tasting caviar was that it's just like lumpy sperm. It has the same flavour, the same slipperiness. It's also exotic and expensive. No wonder it's prized as an aphrodisiac! Eat caviar in dollops on buttered dark rye bread or wholemeal crackers; wash it down with champagne.

Part of my research for this book involved asking my friends about their sexiest meals. A publisher who must remain anonymous told me about his sensuous evenings with his mistress, which usually start with a favourite light supper: smoked salmon, fresh crusty French bread and butter, and champagne. My friend and his lady enjoy this simple repast with a background of soft music, say Mozart or one of the Romantic composers. The food is just sufficient to satisfy hunger and provide the energy necessary for an evening of love-making. It's a light meal that you can enjoy as a picnic in a rose garden in the perfumed summer dusk. It requires little preparation, minimal fuss; it does not distract from the essential purpose of the occasion. With its contrasts of flavour and texture, it stimulates the senses without being overwhelming.

Smoked salmon, like the best lovers' foods, is something you can feed delicately to one another, placing slivers of fish on each other's tongue to savour. It satisfies without making you feel heavy. And it has the sort of flavour that delights but does not linger too long or interfere with the taste of your lover's kisses.

On a more everyday level, fish is one of the best foods you can offer to your lover. Versatile, delicious and nutritious, fish is immensely popular in southern Europe, where it's prepared with much more imagination than in most British restaurants. But even that traditional English dish, fish and chips, can make an erotic feast. Eating fresh fish from paper as you walk in the open air, close to your lover, you can conjure up fabulous dreams of sexual delight, your energies sustained by that simple well-balanced meal. For those of us who are not so young, strolling along the sea-wall eating fish and chips can bring back memories of half-forgotten holiday romances.

The people of that most sexually liberated nation, Holland, are lovers of raw herring, served very fresh and filleted with onions in bread rolls. Their diet of herrings protects the Dutch people from heart disease, keeping their bodies in the good health that is essential to sexual competence. Silky smooth, raw herring can be a sensual feast. But it has to be very fresh indeed.

In Scotland, the kippered herring is believed to have aphrodisiac properties. In his youth, Colin used to take a pair of kippers to parties for a half-time reviver: he's convinced of their potency. I spoke to a charming Edinburgh lady from the Sea Fish Authority who assured me that everyone in her office agreed that kippers made the best breakfast for a relaxed, sensual day; they create an atmosphere conducive to sexual delights. Nobody was willing to describe personal experience, but the conviction was certainly there! Kippers, she explained, are very rich in vitamins, including vitamin E, as well as minerals and essential fatty acids; and, coming from the sea, they incorporate the virtues of the Goddess Aphrodite.

More elaborate fish dishes suit a different sort of occasion; they require that you sit down at table, eating more formally. I recall a Mediterranean-style seafood stew prepared by a man for whom my desire was almost uncontrollable; we watched each other as we ate, itching to caress, holding back only because we had company. Lust grew as we ate, awaiting the opportunity to be alone together. The flavours were most conducive, the occasion desperately frustrating!

Fish stew is a versatile dish that's equally good for special occasions and everyday eating. Wine, shrimps, shellfish and cream make it exotic; prepared simply with coley it's tasty, nourishing, and very healthy. My version of seafood stew (see recipe, page 70) is regularly greeted with astonished delight. It can be made in endless variety, but the basic ingredients are always the same: celery, leeks, tomatoes, carrots, potatoes and fish. Each of these vegetables is said to have aphrodisiac properties, which should enhance the health-promoting qualities of the fish; in combination, they're delicious. I use coley for my fish stew because it's readily available and it stays in meaty chunks. Mullet is also suitable, if more trouble. The stew will be more exotic if you add peeled shrimps, cooked mussels, clams, scallops, or a mixture of these. You can also add a greater variety of vegetables if you wish: peas, shallots, and peppers are good.

Seafood Stew

Imperial/Metric		American
	1 leek, cut into ¼-inch slices	
	1 stick/stalk of celery, cut into ¼-inch slices	
	2 tbs sunflower oil	
	1 large or 2 medium potatoes, peeled and diced	
	1 carrot, sliced	
	3 or 4 ripe tomatoes (canned will do, though fresh are better), chopped	
	1 tbs tomato purée/paste	
1 pt/570ml	vegetable stock or	2½ cups
¾ pt/425ml	stock plus	2 cups
¼ pt/140ml	dry white wine	⅔ cup
	1 tbs chopped parsley	
	1 bay leaf	
	salt to taste	
12 oz/340g	fish and shellfish (coley, mullet, hake, shrimps, prawns, mussels, clams, scallops; subject to taste and availability), skinned and boned	¾ lb
	black pepper	
	cream to taste (optional)	

- Heat the oil in a heavy pot and gently fry the leek and celery until soft.
- Add the potato and carrot; continue frying for a couple of minutes.
- Add the tomatoes and purée.
- Pour in the stock with the herbs and salt, and bring mixture to a boil.
- Cover and simmer until the vegetables are cooked but not disintegrating.

- Skin and bone the fish. Add it with the wine and plenty of pepper to the cooking pot.
- Boil for five minutes or so until the fish is tender.
- If desired, pour in cream to thicken. Serve hot with chilled white wine to accompany the meal.

Fish are the only wild creatures that we are likely to eat. Perhaps it's because they're wild that they embody such sensuous qualities. I dream of the movement of fish as they swim through clear water: how smooth they are, how their bodies glisten. Perhaps some deep part of me longs to return to the sea, from whence we all originated . . . But all we can do is take some of the sea back into ourselves, and with it some of the magic of Aphrodite.

—6—

Red-blooded

Male

*A*sk the majority of men what food they think is most important for sexual potency, and they'll say red meat. Steak is definitely favourite. But can flesh-eating actually inflame the lusts of the flesh?

The association between meat meals and sexual activity goes back a long way into our pre-history. Man the hunter would leave the predominantly vegetarian group of female gatherers to track wild beasts; groups of men might go away for days at a time, as nomadic hunters still do in those parts of the world where their way of life still survives, returning only when the hunt is successful.

Like a pack of wild animals, human men would drag the carcass back to the tribe, where the women would cook a celebratory feast. There'd be enough meat, and more, for everyone, but the men returning hungry from the hunt would get the choicest cuts. After feasting, they'd sleep; and on waking, reach for their womenfolk.

Today's hunk of steak can trigger deeply buried memories of our ancestral world. The hunt may be metaphorical: today's hunters operate in the office and the factory, using their strength and power to generate the income that pays for meat. Women, of course, work and earn too – I'd be the last to deny the feminist revolution! They've always been busy as gatherers, nurturers and agriculturalists. But the kill was, and still is, the man's task; and our minds and bodies remain basically the same as those of our forebears.

Those who eat meat every day may not appreciate its special qualities, but occasional meat-eaters get a definite charge from it. Eating the muscles of animals, we incorporate their strength into our own bodies, gaining something of the qualities, the energies of the creatures who nourish us. Using the nutrients in meat, we re-build and re-vitalize our bodies; the protein and minerals provide the wherewithal to create muscle.

Meat is the richest source of that crucial mineral, zinc, in most people's diets. After oysters, steak provides more zinc than any other food. I've already explained the crucial role of zinc for sexual development and performance; many people, particularly smokers and those who are prone to infections, suffer from some degree of zinc deficiency. Eating red meat can help correct this problem.

I'm not saying we must eat meat for sexual health: far from it. My years of research into health has convinced me that we should not eat meat every day; meat-eating is associated with higher levels of heart disease and cancers; vegetarians are generally considerably healthier than carnivores. Quite apart from that, frequent meat-eating does not make ecological sense. But unless we do make sure that we get sufficient zinc from other sources, whether they be oysters or nuts (see Chapter 8), we will not be able to enjoy our sexuality as much as we could.

Many men and some women find they notice a change in the way they feel when they give up eating meat; a few experience cravings for meat and a renewed sense of well-being when they include an occasional meat meal in a predominantly vegetarian lifestyle. For most people, meat should be a treat, not an everyday food.

That's how I believe we were designed to live, at least in temperate parts of the world. Northern humans evolved through the stress of the last Ice Age, when survival depended on hunting. Today, there are large areas of northern and upland countryside which are incapable of supporting people except through meat production. Where I live and farm in Wales, the pasture would not be capable of sustaining the demands of repeated ploughing and arable farming; the ecosystem is based on grass, shrubs and trees; it's animal food, which feeds those humans who look after and prey on the animals.

Meat-eating is, of course, a very controversial issue. If you're preparing dinner for someone you fancy but don't know well, you must be very careful not to assume that she or he is a carnivore. One in ten are now vegetarian, and the proportion is growing fast, especially among young people. Young women are changing to vegetarianism faster than any other group. Shocked by the cruelties and wastefulness of intensive meat production, more and more people make a moral decision to reject the system and refuse to eat meat.

But not all meat is produced with cruelty; not all farm animals are kept confined, dosed with drugs and hormones, or exposed to pesticides. Increasing numbers of farmers are turning against conventional, chemically-dependent methods of rearing animals.

Organic meat is produced on farms where the welfare of the animals is paramount; where their natural life-cycles are not distorted. On organic farms, birds and other wildlife thrive in unsprayed hedgerows; animals roam over health-giving, herb-rich pastures; and the happiness of the stock is monitored by caring people right up to the brief moment of their slaughter. They're never exposed to the stressful miseries of markets or the callous behaviour of people who have become desensitized to the suffering of animals.

Not surprisingly, the meat from these contented, naturally-reared animals tastes better than its conventional equivalent. It's more expensive and harder to find, but to my mind it's worth the hunt. When you eat organic, you can eat meat with a clear conscience. So, unless you can go to an organic restaurant, organic meat will be something you cook at home when you want the best. Information on where to find organic meat and restaurants is available from the *Thorsons Organic Consumer Guide*, edited by David Mabey and Alan and Jackie Gear (Thorsons, 1990).

Red wine is the perfect accompaniment to red meat, and when the two are cooked together the results are marvellous. So my first recipe, called *Sofrito* (see page 76) is for a very simple steak in red wine and garlic sauce that never goes wrong. Choose meat that's dark in colour, not bright red; it will have more flavour and it's more likely to be tender. You don't need especially good steak for this; I use bladebone.

Sofrito

Imperial/Metric		American
2 oz/55g	butter	¼ cup
	4 cloves garlic, chopped	
¾ lb/340g	steak, coated in seasoned flour	12 oz
	1 tbs flour	
	1 bay leaf	
	6 oz glass red wine (Côtes du Rhône is good)	
¼ pt/140ml	vegetable stock	⅔ cup
	salt and pepper to taste	

- Heat the butter in a heavy frying pan and gently sauté the garlic.
- Add the steak and brown on both sides. When browned remove it from the pan; place it in a casserole dish.
- Add the flour to the butter and meat juices in the frying pan.
- Add the bay leaf and the liquids and bring to the boil, stirring continuously.
- Season to taste.
- Pour this sauce over the steak.
- Cook covered at 350°F/180°C (Gas Mark 4) for about an hour or until very tender.
- Serve with baked or creamed potatoes and seasonal vegetables.

This is a dish that can be cooked gently for a relatively long time; it doesn't impose its time-scale on you. So if you suspect you may not be able to keep your hands off each other after the preparation period, you can just turn the oven down and concentrate on making love! The meal will be just as delicious when you've satisfied your sexual appetite.

Although Sofrito is delightful, beef in Roquefort sauce (recipe page 79) has a particularly sexy flavour. I first tasted it in a restaurant in Amsterdam. We were with dear friends and occasional lovers who were associated with the underground magazine *Suck*, the first European sexpaper. It was a most unusual publication; put together by a group of anarchistic intellectuals which included Jim Haynes, feminist Germaine Greer, poet and playwright Heathcote Williams, and writer/alternative publisher Bill Levy, it celebrated sex in all its variations in a very colourful and personal way. I was eager to meet *Suck* writer and distributor Bill Daley after reading his tender and intimate descriptions of sexual dalliances; the experiences I was to share with him were totally memorable for their intense joy. It was he who led us to this particular restaurant for a special meal.

Many people will imagine that sex magazine publishers are cynical men out to exploit other people's loneliness. Some are; those purveyors of soft porn who portray women only as sex objects to be used by emotionally dead men, perpetrating attitudes and assumptions that divide the sexes and degrade sex: these people do exist. The dullness of their products reveals their own lack of human understanding.

The editors of *Suck* were entirely different. They organized and participated in sex festivals in Amsterdam which were recorded in books beautifully designed by Dutch artist and broadcaster Willem de Ridder; the *Wet Dream Book* is one of the loveliest products of 70s alternative publishing. Unfortunately British obscenity laws prevent these beautiful, honest and touching books from reaching England.

For the very special people who created *Suck*, sex was something to be celebrated, explored and enjoyed to the full. Shame and guilt didn't come into it. I fell in love with more than one of them; the pleasure was exquisite, the partings inevitably painful.

'Seek new perfumes, larger blossoms, pleasures still untasted,' wrote Bill Levy in his anthology, *Natural Jewboy*. I cannot quote extensively from its pages in this relatively respectable publication; all I can offer is a brief taste of Bill's poetic style. 'Flesh heating flesh . . . our bodies dance and glow. I am no longer in control. My body ripples with movements directed by the inner logic of its own ecstasy. A flush of warmth spreads through my whole body . . .'

Bill is now married to fellow editor Purple Susan. I am settled in a Welsh farm with Colin, my long-time partner. But such passion as we experienced never dies completely. However . . . 'Let us move on to concrete events, which are transformed by the soul into absolute and divine experiences.'

To a small Amsterdam restaurant, and steak in Roquefort sauce. The softly lit table was covered with a fine carpet in the Dutch manner; in the background, a pianist played jazz. As we ate, the flavour of the meat in its luscious sauce reminded me of the salty taste of Bill's lean body. Which Bill? It could have been either, I loved them both . . .

Steak in Roquefort Sauce

Imperial/Metric		American
	Marinade:	
	4 tbs oil	
	4 tbs wine	
	1 or 2 cloves garlic, crushed	
	chopped herbs to taste	
	Steak Roquefort:	
¼ pt/140ml	white wine	⅔ cup
¼ pt/140ml	beef stock	⅔ cup
1 lb/455g	top-quality beef steak – rump,	1 lb
	sirloin or fillet	
1 oz/30g	butter	2 tbs
	1 level tbs flour or cornflour/cornstarch	
	pepper to taste	
3 oz/85g	Roquefort cheese	¾ cup
¼ pt/140ml	double/heavy cream	⅔ cup

● Make up the marinade by mixing the oil, wine, garlic and herbs together. Cover the raw meat with the marinade and leave it in the refrigerator for at least six hours – ideally you should make up the marinade the day before you plan to eat the meal.

● When you're ready to start cooking, remove the meat from the marinade mixture and set it aside to dry.

● Boil the wine and stock together in an open pan until reduced to about half volume.

● Grill the meat for just 2 to 4 minutes per side: the shorter the cooking time, the rarer the steak.

● Put the steak aside on a warm plate while you make the sauce.

● Melt the butter in a saucepan large enough to take the meat. Remove from the heat and stir in the flour.

● Pour on the reduced liquor and add any juices from the grill, stirring steadily to remove any lumps.

- Return to the heat and boil for one minute till thickened. Season with pepper (salt won't be necessary).
- Add the steak to the pan to continue cooking for a further 2 to 4 minutes.
- Crumble the cheese and stir it into the liquid in the pan. Heat gently – do *not* boil – for 2 minutes.
- Serve with fresh green vegetables and creamed potatoes.

Carpetbag steak (see recipe below) is a stuffed beef roll which you can shape into a monster phallus. The traditional stuffing is made with oysters, which will contribute their unique aphrodisiac qualities to the meal.

Carpetbag Steak

Imperial/Metric		*American*
1 oz/30g	butter	2 tbs
2 oz/55g	sliced mushrooms	¾ cup
	10 small oysters, sliced	
2 oz/60g	soft breadcrumbs	1 cup
	1 tbs chopped parsley	
	salt and pepper to taste	
	juice of ½ lemon	
	1 egg, beaten	
1 lb/455g	steak in one large thin piece	1 lb
	(beat out a smaller piece with a	
	wooden mallet if necessary)	
1 oz/30g	butter	2 tbs

- Heat the first portion of the butter; add the mushroom and fry them until they are nearly cooked through.
- Add the oysters and cook for a further 2 to 3 minutes.

- Stir in the breadcrumbs, parsley, seasoning and lemon juice; bind together with beaten egg. This is your stuffing.
- Roll the steak into a thick phallus around the stuffing and secure by stitching together or pinning with cocktail sticks.
- Spread the steak with the remaining butter and roast for about half an hour, starting in a hot oven – 425°F/220°C (Gas Mark 7) – for 15 minutes and then reducing the temperature to complete the cooking.
- Serve with boiled potatoes coated with butter, arranged suggestively either side of the meat, accompanied with salad.

You can cut into this steak with relish: is it a threat or a suggestive act when you lift the pieces to your lips?

My next meat recipe is for *Coq au vin* (see page 83). The name itself is suggestive, but for me the sexual connotations are related to the nature of the cockerel. The cock is an intensely sexy creature; indeed, sex is his total *raison d'être*. Don't buy a frozen bird produced on a conventional chicken farm: there's nothing sexy about that environment, and your bird just won't taste good enough to justify the trouble you're going to.

Although you can make Coq au vin with chicken, a real cockerel is much better. Even so-called free-range chickens are usually fed such unsuitable food that they are relatively flavourless. So find someone who rears chickens in a garden or farmyard where they're free to scratch to their hearts' content, eating as much green stuff as they want, as well as all the insects, grubs and snails they enjoy.

My first cockerel lived in our back garden; we'd reared him with the hens since they were all day-old chicks, and I grew inordinately fond of him. He would emerge from the hen-house in the morning and dance around me, prancing sideways with one wing extended, flirting wildly. To me he was totally affectionate; to others, a terror. His twin obsessions were protecting and bonking the hens; unfortunately he was so dedicated to both of these activities that we were unable to keep him.

By the time he was a little over a year old, the hens had lost all the feathers from their backs where he would hold on to them with his claws and beak as he satisfied his excessive sexual urges. A magnificent Rhode Island Red, he stood well over two feet tall and when he flew at people, they were justifiably scared. Both our neighbours and the postman became terrified of his attacks. So my sexy cockerel had to go, though his feathers grew damp with my tears as I plucked him. Cooked with all the care due such a special creature, he became Coq au vin, and very delicious he was too.

I imagine that the chicken legs that Albert Finney and Joyce Redman devoured in the film *Tom Jones* could only have been so devastatingly sexy if they had come from a cockerel. It was an intensely memorable scene; seated opposite one another at a table groaning with food, the would-be lovers licked and tore at the meat in the most suggestive way. They held the drumsticks with their fingers – no niceties of cutlery, the direct connection is so much more erotic!

Does the sexiness of the cock transfer to us when we eat him? Maybe, in some measure, his spirit continues. Surely it can be no coincidence that he goes by the same name as one appellation for the male member.

Although this recipe can include bacon as I have written it here, I usually have to leave the bacon out because I can't get organic bacon locally, and I refuse to support the conventional pig-production units, even to the extent of buying a few rashers of their inferior meat. Bacon is not essential to Coq au vin, but it does improve the flavour.

Coq au Vin

Imperial/Metric		American
	2 tbs cooking oil	
	1 free-range cockerel or chicken (4lb/1800g/4lb or more), cut into portion-sized pieces	
	3 rashers/slices of bacon	
	2 sticks/stalks of celery, chopped	
	2 cloves garlic, crushed	
	2 tbs flour	
¾ pt/425ml	red wine	2 cups
	1 bay leaf	
	bouquet garni	
	salt and pepper	
2 oz/55g	butter	¼ cup
6 oz/170g	small (pickling) onions, chopped	1 cup
6 oz/170g	mushrooms, chopped	2¼ cups

- Heat the oil in a large flameproof casserole, add the chicken and brown all over.
- When fully browned remove the chicken from the casserole.
- Put the bacon, celery and garlic in the hot casserole and fry until the bacon is crisp.
- Stir in the flour to form a paste.
- Gradually add the wine, herbs and seasoning, stirring continuously. Bring to the boil.
- Return the chicken to the casserole, cover and cook at 325°F/ 170°C (Gas Mark 3) for approx one hour: less if your chicken weighs four pounds or under, more for a well-grown bird.
- Fry the onions and mushrooms in the butter for 5 minutes.
- Add the onions and mushrooms to the casserole, replace the lid and continue cooking for another three-quarters of an hour, or until the chicken is tender.

This dish will serve at least four people, and up to ten if you've found a Rhode Island Red or similar full-sized cockerel. But if there's just the two of you sharing an intimate dinner, you won't need to waste any; Coq au vin freezes well.

My final recipe comes from the West Indies (see page 85). It used to be cooked for me on Sunday afternoons by Jimmy, a karate champion from Barbados who would roam around his flat in a short bathrobe. He took pleasure in demonstrating his amazing strength and agility by kicking and leaping into the air with the most muscular legs I have ever seen, revealing a tantalizing glimpse of naked buttock. He was a very physical man, who didn't talk much. But that was all right by me; our relationship wasn't about talking.

I don't know how far the hot pepper sauce with the chicken spiced up our interaction; but I do know now that peppers and spices are believed by people of many different cultures to have aphrodisiac properties. Was Jimmy aware of this? Certainly by the time he'd finished cooking and cavorting, and we'd eaten the delicious product of his labours, we would always be hot for each other!

Karate Chicken

Imperial/Metric		American
	1 small chicken	
	seasoned flour as needed	
	3 tbs cooking oil	
	2 cloves garlic, chopped	
	1 onion, chopped	
	2 red peppers, pith and seeds removed	
8 oz/225g	tomatoes, canned or fresh, chopped	1⅓ cup
	½ hot chilli pepper, seeded and chopped	
	1 tsp allspice	
	½ tsp paprika	
	salt and black pepper	

- Joint or bone the meat (you can use lamb or rabbit in place of chicken if you prefer) and cut into good-sized chunks. Roll in seasoned flour.
- Heat the oil in a flameproof casserole or heavy pan and fry the meat along with the garlic until browned. Remove the meat.
- Add the onion and peppers and sauté until soft.
- Add the tomatoes along with the spices and seasonings.
- Return the meat to the pot, cover and cook gently in the oven at 325°F/170°C (Gas Mark 3), or simmer on the stove for an hour or until the meat is tender. Check at intervals to see that it doesn't get dry, adding water if necessary.
- Serve with boiled rice or roast potatoes and vegetables.

I hope this dish brings as much pleasure to you as it did to Jimmy and me!

—7—

Fruity

Passions

*A*dam and Eve had no awareness of themselves as sexual beings before they ate the forbidden apple. The Bible says: 'When the woman saw that the tree was good for food, and that it was a delight to the eyes, and that the tree was desired to make one wise, she took of the fruit thereof, and did eat; and she gave also unto her husband with her, and he did eat. And the eyes of them both were opened, and they knew that they were naked' (Genesis 1: 6-7). Thus the apple was given a special place in mythology as the fruit of temptation and of knowledge.

In Greek mythology, apples were sacred to Aphrodite (along with roses, poppies and the myrtle). 'You are the apple of my eye,' we may say, offering rosy fruit in a gesture that carries implications of desire. Red or golden, apples are symbols of fruitfulness, of fulfilment. I can't say the same for the green varieties that are so popular in our shops; but they aren't chosen for their sensual qualities!

To me, apples aren't the sexiest fruit. They're somehow too fresh, too crunchy and wholesome, more reminiscent of healthy open-air sport than the musky sport of the bedroom. Apples are for keeping your breath fresh, your teeth sparkling. You might crunch them before meeting your lover, or for pleasure just as often as you fancy, but I don't feel they have any special sexual connotations.

Now maybe my attitude is a bit peculiar, because I eat a great many apples and I see them as everyday fare. Perhaps apples used in the traditional Newfoundland lovers' way, pricked full of holes and held in the armpit so that they absorb the smell of the body, would have more sex-appeal.

Fruit can be very erotic, and many types of fruit are reputed to have aphrodisiac effects. Fruit plays an important part in the good sex diet because it provides vitamins A and C, along with important minerals such as Boron. It keeps our bodies from growing sluggish, giving energy in its most accessible form.

What makes fruit really special is that it's the one food that's designed by nature purely for eating (apart, that is, from milk; but that's meant only for young animals, the offspring of the mother). The plant produces fruit, making it appealing to the eye, delicious and tender to the lips, so that animals such as ourselves should be tempted to pluck and consume it, thus moving embedded seeds away from the parent plant. We are co-operating with the plant, playing our part in its efforts to reproduce. And the plant rewards us with pleasure in the sweetness and succulence of its fruit.

The Chinese and the Arabs are very tuned in to the sexiness of fruit. They regard peaches, in particular, as aphrodisiacs; the deep downy cleft and the rosy bloom of the peach are symbolic of female sex organs. 'Peach house' used to be the Chinese slang term for brothel; a peach is a pretty, sexy girl. In Japan, the peach is a symbol of fertility.

Peaches are the most sensual fruits. Their soft skin, tender, easily bruised, has the texture of the most delicate and sensitive skin. As you bite into a peach, its sweet juice runs over your face like the secretions of your lover's arousal; their luscious flesh is smooth, pink and silky like genitalia. Peaches don't need any preparation; choose them ripe and they're perfect for the sexiest snack or the finishing touch to your erotic meal.

The flesh of ripe, yielding fruit carries connotations of the mature sensual woman. Mangoes and melons, especially those with sweet rosy flesh, bring out the sensuality in the eater. Let the juices run over your lips, to be kissed away by your lover. Mangoes, like peaches, are traditional aphrodisiacs; melons are frequently compared to women's breasts, rich and full.

When you are choosing fruit for its erotic potential, always look for ripeness. The best way to judge whether any piece of fruit is ready is by smelling it; ripe fruit has a sweet, rich perfume that hints of its delicious flavour. If you can barely smell anything, the fruit is of poor quality or not ready to eat; it will lack flavour and juiciness. This is a much more reliable method of selection than pressing fruit in the hope of judging its ripeness, and it does not damage the fruit.

Bananas are sexy by virtue of their phallic shape. But there's more to them than this; they are also highly nutritious. Rich in vitamin B_6, bananas are especially valuable for women in the second half of their monthly cycle, when they can help to ward off the pre-menstrual blues.

Watching a woman eating a banana can be an incredible come-on for a man; as she licks and nibbles at the shaft of the banana he can dream of her lips around him: the connection is immediate, the fantasy complete. For her, as she consumes the banana, the dream is of consuming him, taking his substance into herself, absorbing him totally. From the shared dream, you can create a shared experience of sexual indulgence.

Not surprisingly, old-fashioned books on etiquette emphasize that one should never eat a banana in this manner. There's nothing quite as cold as etiquette, with its deliberate suppression of suggestive behaviour, its rejection of sensuality. Bananas, according to such authorities, should be sliced with a knife, eaten with a fork – just in case anyone watching should get any erotic charge from it! But sex isn't ladylike; I'm talking about liberating the real you, forgetting the ice-maiden. In the bedroom, or when we are creating the atmosphere of the bedroom, we do not behave in a respectable manner. The sensual lover breaks all those rules, exploiting the erotic potential of food to the full.

Bananas with whipped cream can be even more suggestive, though they're more difficult to eat in an erotic manner. But the combination of bananas and cream is reminiscent of the excited male, ready for action.

Add a couple of scoops of ice-cream either side of the phallic shape of the banana, decorate the tip with cream, and you have a dish that could not be more explicit. Alternatively, if you cut the banana lengthwise and lie both halves, their tips touching, on a bed of chocolate sauce, the visual turn-on changes to one suggesting a vulva. Decorate the centre with a cherry to focus the eye and mind, and you produce a totally unambiguous statement of availability. Perhaps you should serve one dish of each, to complement one another!

In the inner skin of the banana there's a drug, the alkaloid *bufotenine*, which some authorities believe to have aphrodisiac properties. A couple of decades ago, a craze swept California for smoking banana skins; but this didn't prove to be a particularly effective way of enjoying the effects of bufotenine. A better way is to bake ripe bananas in their skins (see recipe below).

Banana Delight

Imperial/Metric		*American*
	2 ripe bananas	
3 oz/85g	dark brown sugar	½ cup
	½ tsp Jamaican allspice	
	single/light cream as needed	

- Slit the bananas lengthwise and fill the cuts with dark brown sugar.
- Cook in the oven at 350°F/180°C (Gas Mark 4) for 20 minutes.
- Remove the skins, scrape them out and mix the scrapings with the juices from the cooked bananas.
- Pour juice over the bananas, sprinkle with Jamaican allspice, and serve with cream.

The cherry is another fruit that's often linked with sex. A girl's cherry, of course, is her virginity: small, sweet, and red. Cherries are perfect for popping into each other's mouths, creating intimacy through sharing.

In scenes of erotic indulgence, the fruit that features again and again is the grape. Bunches of grapes, the fruits of Dionysus, are suspended lusciously over lovers' lips in romantic paintings; they spill from cornucopia in feast scenes. Grapes signify pleasure and plenty.

'Peel me a grape,' demands Mae West in her most suggestive manner; in its soft juicy nakedness, the peeled purple grape induces thoughts of our most vulnerable parts. As you drop peeled grapes between your lover's waiting lips, you are offering yourself in the most intimate way.

Figs, too, are fruits of indulgence, when they're sweet and ripe and gummy, the skin purple, the flesh red and gold. In Ken Russell's film of D.H. Lawrence's *Women in Love*, Alan Bates, playing the part of Rupert, eats a fig and explains why they've been credited with aphrodisiac properties:

> *The proper way to eat a fig in society is to split it in four, holding it by the stump, and open it so that it is a glittering rosy moist honeyed heavy-petalled, four-petalled flower. Then you throw away the skin after you have taken off the blossom with your lips. But the vulgar way is just to put your mouth to the crack and take out the flesh in one bite.*
>
> *The fig is a very secretive fruit. The Italians vulgarly say it stands for the female part, the fig fruit; the fissure, the yoni. The wonderful moist conductivity towards the centre, involved, inturned, one small way of access only and this close curtained from the light. Sap that smells strange on your fingers, so that even goats won't taste it. And when the fig has kept her secret long enough, it explodes and you see through the fissure, the scarlet. And the fig is finished. The year is over. That's how the fig dies, showing her crimson through*

the purple slit. Like a wound, the exposure of her secret on the open day; like a prostitute, the bursting fig makes a show of her secret.

Watching this remarkable film, I realize that my anti-TV views definitely do not apply to erotic videos! I am resolved to build up a collection of erotic classics. They can be a marvellous way to get turned on to sexual delights; the scene where Alan Bates wrestles naked with Oliver Reed gets me going every time I see it. And Glenda Jackson is certainly to Colin's taste.

Whatever fruit you prefer, it will make the perfect complement for a lover's feast. A carefully arranged dish of fruit can make a lovely centre for your table, ready to refresh the most jaded palate. And when your mouth feels dry after a sexual extravaganza, there's nothing to equal fruit for refreshing your spirits, replenishing the juices, and re-vitalizing your energy stores for another bout. Take fruit with you to the bedroom for post-coital indulgence, and see how fruity kisses can draw you together again!

—8—
Nuts
About Nuts

Some years ago, I was given a lewd little nutcracker. Made of brass, it's in the shape of a pair of female legs, with the hinge at the crotch. If ever I needed a reminder of the links between nuts and sex, that nutcracker is it! The question that lingers is the significance of the gift: 'nutcracker' has a variety of meanings . . .

Some meanings of the word 'nut' reflect different aspects of the nut in its original sense as in the fruit of the nut-tree: *Nuts*, slang for testicles, carry a man's germ plasm, just as nuts carry the tree's; *nutty* in the sense of crazy, is an appropriate word for people in the wild throes of love; and *'going a-nutting'* once meant love-making, for licentious revels used to be associated with gathering hazelnuts in country districts of England. Is there an untold side of Beatrix Potter's story *Squirrel Nutkin* that's unsuitable for children?

Nuts are very special foods. Most people think of them as snacks and don't take them seriously as an important part of the diet; but this attitude isn't justified. In fact, nuts are the richest sources of nutrients you can get. Different types vary in the balance of particular micro-nutrients they contain, but most nuts are chock-full of minerals that the Western diet often lacks, such as magnesium, iron, zinc, potassium, phosphorus and calcium. They're rich in vitamins, too, particularly the good sex vitamin, tocopherol (vitamin E). They contain the sulphur-rich amino acids that we need for beautiful thick hair, strong nails and healthy skin, as well as for protection from environmental pollution. And they contain health-promoting essential fatty acids.

When I was working on one of our earlier books, *Alternatives to Drugs* (Fontana), I found myself recommending Brazil nuts more often than any other single food, because of the high concentration of valuable nutrients they contain. Whatever your health problem, it seems, Brazil nuts are part of the answer.

Almonds, hazelnuts and sunflower seeds are particularly rich sources of vitamin E. Brazil nuts and almonds are richest in magnesium; Brazils and walnuts have the highest levels of phosphorus and zinc. Cashews and Brazils are the best sources of those sulphur-rich amino acids.

So nuts are essential components of the good sex diet. Really, there's nothing better than nuts for your sex-life! A dish of mixed nuts and seeds is the most nutritious snack; nuts are good for everyday as well as for special occasions. They need no preparation, they keep well – nuts are nature's convenience food. Why don't we eat more of them?

While hazel or cob nuts were associated with fertility in England, almonds feature in aphrodisiac recipes from all over the world. They are regarded as symbols of fertility, and indeed their value for regulating female hormones means their benefits are far more than symbolic. Many women who suffer from pre-menstrual tension (PMT) – and that includes three-quarters of all women of child-bearing age – may lose interest in sex for up to two weeks in each month before the menstrual period begins. Eating nuts is a delightful and effective way of reducing PMT and thus reviving sexual desire during those weeks.

You can enjoy almonds raw, roasted, or in dishes ranging from savoury nut roasts to nut breads and marzipan (see recipe, page 113).

Nuts are also so versatile, they can form part of any meal. They're good with cereals for breakfast, as nut butter on toast, in biscuits with your morning coffee, in lunchtime savouries. They're delicious in cakes and tea-breads, delightful in dinner dishes, and they make the perfect after-dinner snack.

Use nuts as your protein source when you're cooking a meal for a lover who's vegetarian or vegan; nuts contain as much protein as meat, fish or cheese. And unlike the other main sources of vegetable protein, beans and peas, nuts won't make you flatulent! Which is a definite advantage when you are planning a romantic evening.

In Greece, almonds are symbols of happiness; in Italy of fidelity. For this reason sugared almonds feature at weddings in both these countries; and almonds are sought after particularly by unmarried girls. According to traditional lore, a girl who puts one of these almonds under her pillow at night will dream of the man who is to be her husband.

Macaroons (see recipe, page 95) are one of my favourite ways of preparing almonds for an energy-enhancing snack that's equally good at midnight or when you're luxuriating in a long, sensuous lie-in in the morning. You have to be careful what you eat in bed. Toast crumbs are horribly itchy, while anything sticky or sloppy is liable to make a dreadful mess of the sheets. Macaroons are ideal; the crumbs are quite small and they go soft without getting greasy or gluey so you can just shake them out when you finally rise.

Almond Macaroons

Imperial/Metric		American
	rice paper as needed	
6 oz/170g	ground almonds	2¼ cups
1 oz/30g	icing/confectioner's sugar	¼ cup
7 oz/200g	sugar	1¼ cups
	1 tsp ground rice	
	3 egg-whites, lightly beaten	
	almond essence/extract	
	3 dozen almonds, halved and blanched	

- Pre-heat the oven to 300°F/150°C (Gas Mark 2).
- Line two large baking sheets with rice paper.
- Mix the ground almonds with the two kinds of sugar and ground rice. Stir in the egg whites and a few drops of almond essence and mix very thoroughly.
- Drop spoonfuls of the mixture onto rice paper, allowing plenty of room for the biscuits to expand during cooking. Top each one with half a blanched almond.
- Bake for half an hour, or until the biscuits are a light golden brown.
- When the macaroons are cool, strip off the rice paper surrounding each biscuit. Store in an airtight tin.

Walnuts are excellent in sophisticated cooked dishes. You can use them in stuffings, salads, sauces, cakes and puddings. One of my favourite walnut dishes is an unusual pasta mixture which makes a light and tasty but nourishing main dish for lunch or supper (see recipe, page 96). Serve it with a mixed salad.

Pasta with Broccoli and Walnuts

The quantities for this dish are very flexible; you can vary them according to personal taste.

Imperial/Metric		American
6 oz/170g	wholewheat pasta (spirals, bows or similar shapes)	3 cups
8 oz/225g	broccoli	8 oz
1 oz/30g	butter	2 tbs
2 oz/55g	walnuts, coarsely chopped	½ cup
1 oz/30g	anchovies	1 oz
2 oz/55g	mature Cheddar cheese, finely grated or	½ cup
	1½ oz freshly grated Parmesan	
	1 tbs parsley	
	salt and black pepper to taste	

- Boil the pasta in plenty of salted water until just tender. Drain and set aside in a warm place.
- Boil the broccoli for as short a time as possible: if the pieces are small and fresh, they only need to be boiled for about one minute. Drain.
- Melt the butter in a heavy pan and stir in the broccoli, walnuts and anchovies; cook gently for 2 minutes.
- Stir in the pasta and warm through, shaking the pan over the heat so the mixture does not burn.
- Remove from heat; stir in the cheese, parsley, salt and black pepper. Serve hot.

The crunchiness of walnuts makes them ideal for salads. Try mixing walnuts with a few chopped dried unsulphured apricots and grated sweet winter swede/squash or carrots; or with chopped celery, apple, red pepper and mayonnaise.

Eat walnuts in the afternoon in a delicious banana tea-bread (see recipe below). Do try to get a lemon that hasn't been sprayed with pesticides for this recipe; it will improve the tea-bread's taste and will be much healthier for you. The tea-bread will provide both energy and valuable nourishment to maintain your stamina through any sort of marathon.

Walnut and Banana Tea-bread

Imperial/Metric		American
7 oz/200g	wholemeal flour	1¾ cups
	2 level tsp baking powder	
	pinch of salt	
3 oz/85g	butter or sunflower margarine	⅓ cup
3 oz/85g	soft brown sugar	½ cup
	2 small eggs, beaten	
12 oz/340g	peeled ripe bananas, mashed	2-2¼ cups
	grated rind of 1 lemon	
3 oz/85g	marzipan, roughly chopped into large chunks (see recipe, page 113)	½ cup
2 oz/55g	walnuts, chopped	½ cup
1 oz/30g	walnuts	¼ cup

- Set the oven to 350°F/180°C (Gas Mark 4).
- Line a 2-lb loaf tin with oiled greaseproof paper.
- Sieve the flour with the baking powder and salt.
- Cream the butter with the sugar till light and fluffy, then beat in the eggs.
- Mix in the bananas, lemon rind, marzipan and chopped nuts.
- Turn the mixture into your loaf tin and decorate with the remaining nuts, then bake for about one hour until golden brown.
- When cool, wrap in kitchen foil to keep moist.

You can eat this tea-bread fresh and warm on its own, or spread with butter or margarine. For a feast, serve it soaked in brandy with a dollop of double cream.

The further East you go in the world, the more you encounter nuts in cooked dishes. Nuts and rice are a popular combination from Greece to Japan; try adding roasted cashews and almonds to stir-fried vegetables and rice, well seasoned with Tamari soy sauce.

The ancient Greeks and Romans regarded pine-nuts as aphrodisiacs; Ovid advised lovers to eat them in *De Arte Amoris*. So they definitely deserve a place in the good sex diet! Pine-nuts are used in many Greek and Turkish recipes; they're often mixed with rice in stuffings for leaves or vegetables (see recipe, page 99). Unfortunately, pine nuts can go rancid quite quickly, so make sure you get them fresh.

Pine-Nut Stuffing

Imperial/Metric		American
	2 tbs olive oil	
	2 onions, chopped fine	
	vegetable pulp as needed (courgettes/zucchini, aubergine/eggplant, etc.)	
	2 tomatoes, chopped fine (optional)	
	1 clove garlic, crushed	
4 oz/115g	boiled rice	1 cup
2 oz/55g	pine nuts	½ cup
	1 tbs chopped parsley	
	pinch nutmeg	
	salt and pepper to taste	

This mixture is suitable for wrapping in cabbage or vine leaves, or for stuffing peppers, courgettes/zucchini, aubergines/eggplant or tomatoes.

- Scoop out the pulp from the vegetables; if you are using peppers discard their seeds, but chop and retain all other vegetable pulp. Set the now-empty vegetable cases aside.
- Heat the oil and fry the onions until golden.
- Stir in the vegetable pulp, tomatoes and garlic, and cook for 5 minutes. Add the rice, nuts, parsley, nutmeg and seasonings.
- Fill the empty vegetable cases with this mixture.
- Bake in a well-oiled covered dish in a moderate oven – 350°F/180°C (Gas Mark 4) – for about an hour.

I didn't find any specific mention of cashew nuts in my research into traditional aphrodisiacs, but they're much too delicious and nutritious to leave out! Cashews have a uniquely sweet and subtle flavour. I like them best with apricots – a mixture that provides not only energy but a host of valuable nutrients. Use the sticky brown unsulphured apricots that you can get from good wholefood shops; they taste much better than the bright orange rubbery apricots that seem to be more popular. Unsulphured apricots may not look as good, but that bright colour is produced by treating the fruit with sulphur dioxide or sulphites, which not only spoil the flavour, but also cause nasty headaches and other unpleasant reactions in sensitive people.

The method is very simple. Just open each apricot carefully and stuff it chock-full of cashew pieces. Roll it in fine icing sugar if it's very sticky. Then eat, savouring the contrast of textures and the marvellous combination of flavours. Try not to eat too many – they're awfully more-ish but very filling!

—9—
Vegetable
Pleasures

*T*he shape, colour and size of particular vegetables has caused them to be picked out as good for sexual pleasure. The Greeks called the carrot 'philon', which is derived from the word for loving, because of its shape and colour; and served it to lovers. Yet there are a variety of other reasons that have more to do with food value. Of course, it's impossible to know precisely why aphrodisiac properties are ascribed to particular foods, but it's become clear to me that in most cases, their nutritional characteristics offer real benefits to our sex lives.

The main value of vegetables in the good sex diet is long term. They won't give you the sort of kick-start that stimulant foods such as chocolate can offer, nor do most vegetables provide much short-term energy; but they will keep you in good shape for many years. So one rule of the good sex diet is simply this – eat more vegetables! All sorts of vegetables. Few of us get enough, especially in Britain, where we eat less veggies than anywhere else in Europe.

While all vegetables will help keep you fit for sex, not all are suitable for that special loving lunch or supper. There are some that are reputed to reduce your passion; Aphrodite, it's said, cooled her ardour on a bed of lettuce. Cucumber, despite its phallic shape, is another that isn't recommended. Munching your way through a big green salad may not, therefore, get you going like a rabbit!

Celery, however, is regarded in a different light – many Italian men swear by it. Celery contains a *pheromone*, a substance akin to the sexual scents that attract mates to us, and enhance our own attractiveness. So *crudités* – crisp sticks of raw celery and carrot – could make a good start to your loving meal. And when you're eating crudités, don't neglect the opportunities they offer for suggestive nibbling! The way you eat them can say a lot to your partner.

Once again, I must emphasize the importance of finding sources of organic food. Carrots that have been grown by conventional means may look good, but they have so little flavour, all you get is the crunch. If you haven't tasted organic carrots, seek some out and just compare them with conventionally-grown ones. That's what carrots should taste like; most people put up with a very poor substitute. It's time consumers rebelled against flavourless food!

If you're serving cooked carrots as part of an aphrodisiac meal, make the most of their suggestive shape by keeping them whole. Naturally you'll have to choose carrots of the right shape and size to create the impact you're after. Then, if you want to go over the top, how about placing a scoop of mashed potatoes or swede either side of your phallic carrot?

The recent vogue for carefully presented food, artistically arranged on the plate, never made the most of the opportunities for communication through the medium of food. Maybe that's because serving such blatantly suggestive dishes in restaurants would be taboo. At home, we can reject these conventions and constraints. Your partner might fall about laughing at the vision of veggie genitalia, but that's fine: jokes relax us and release inhibitions. When sex isn't fun, it's not worth doing.

When you prepare carrots consciously as phallic symbols, you are building on an ancient belief that's shared by many different cultures. This is the 'doctrine of signatures', which holds that every plant useful to man was marked by God – or the Goddess – in a way that reveals its intended use. Plants that resemble organs of the body were believed to have particular benefits for those organs. Both carrots and asparagus owe their reputations as aphrodisiacs to this doctrine; but both do, of course, offer real benefits to well-being, and so, to some degree at least, their aphrodisiac reputations are justified.

Some of the aphrodisiac vegetables of Eastern cultures, such as onions and peas, bear no overt resemblance to genital organs, and how their reputations developed I do not know. But I do believe that there are valid reasons for their reputations, reasons that go far beyond the state of theoretical knowledge that existed at that time.

Peas and onions are acknowledged by Western medical experts to reduce cholesterol levels and protect the circulatory system, which is so important for male sexual potency. Peas and beans, and chick-peas (also known as garbanzo beans) in particular, produce a slow release of energy that keeps blood-sugar even and maintains the healthy functioning of your intestines. This can help protect against diabetes, which is an increasingly common cause of impotence in middle-aged and elderly men.

The Perfumed Garden of the Shaykh Nefzawi (tr. Sir Richard Burton, Grafton, 1963) is a rich source of vegetable-based aphrodisiac recipes, although some may seem strange to Western tastes. Many dishes include egg-yolks; all are highly spiced (see Chapter 10 for the aphrodisiac tradition of spices). Here are a few examples of the original recipes and the effects that the Sheik Nefzawi assures his readers they will have:

> *Green peas, boiled carefully with onions, and powdered with cinnamon, ginger and cardamoms, well pounded, create for the consumer considerable amorous passion and strength in coitus.*
>
> *He who boils asparagus, and then fries them in fat, and then pours upon them the yolks of eggs with pounded condiments, and eats every day of this dish, will grow very strong for the coitus, and find in it a stimulant for his amorous desires.*
>
> *He who peels onions, puts them in a saucepan with condiments and aromatic substances, and fries the mixture with oil and yolks of eggs, will acquire a surpassing and invaluable vigour for the coitus, if he will partake of this dish for several days.*

*The member of Abou el Heiloukh has remained erect for thirty days
without a break, because he did eat onions. Abou el Heidja has
deflowered in one night once eighty virgins, and he did not eat or
drink between, because he'd surfeited himself first with chick-peas
and had drunk camel's milk with honey mixed.*

The story of Abou el Heidja reveals that he did not eat onions alone;
the dish included chick-peas and meat with 'an abundance of onions'.

Although *The Perfumed Garden* suggests that these vegetables have
an immediate effect on male sexual stamina, I see them as helping
to keep you fit for sex in the long term, rather than foods you might
choose to prepare for a night of love-making. For people who are
unaccustomed to large quantities of vegetables, eating an abundance
of onions with chick-peas could have effects on the digestive system
that their lovers might find distinctly unappealing!

On page 105 you'll find a recipe that Abou el Heidja might have
found suitable for his hard night's work. It makes a hearty hot-pot
for hungry lovers.

Chick-peas with Meat and Onions

Imperial/Metric   *American*

2 onions, chopped
1 tbs sunflower oil
2 large ripe tomatoes, chopped
1 16-oz can chick-peas or 6 oz dried chick-peas,
soaked and boiled
1 clove garlic, crushed

4 oz/100g   cooked meat, cut into pieces (optional)   ¼ lb

parsley to taste, chopped fine
salt and pepper to taste
tomato juice or stock as needed

Chick-peas take such a long time to cook, they're one of the few vegetables I buy canned. If you prefer to prepare dried chick-peas yourself, you'll need to soak them for 24 hours and then leave them boiling in plenty of water for a further four hours.

- Fry the onions in the oil until soft and golden.
- Add the tomato, drained peas, garlic, and pieces of cooked meat (lamb, pork, garlic sausage or a mixture of meats).
- Stir in the parsley and season to taste with salt and pepper.
- Cover and cook gently for 20 minutes, adding tomato juice or stock if the mixture gets dry.

The Sheik Nefzawi was just one of many writers who believed in the special virtues of asparagus. In the 16th century, John Gerald recorded that 'The young buds being steeped in wine and eaten, they stirreth up the lust of the body.' According to the herbalist Culpeper, 'A decoction of the roots being taken fasting several mornings together, stirreth up bodily lust in man or woman.'

Intriguingly, asparagus, like many other traditional aphrodisiacs, contains a remarkably high proportion of vitamin E, the fertility vitamin. Obviously, none of the herbalists of centuries ago knew anything of this vitamin, but what is apparent is that their observations were valid and their recommendations make sense even in terms of modern science. We would be foolish to dismiss their experience.

I doubt if its vitamin E content is the only aspect of asparagus that's important to its aphrodisiac qualities; in nature, nutrients often occur in complex groups whose total effect is greater than the sum of the parts; nutrients in food act in synergy. Taking a capsule of vitamin E is not likely to do as much for your sex-life as eating asparagus – and it's not nearly so enjoyable, either!

Asparagus is a luxury vegetable but it can be prepared very simply (see recipe below).

Simply Asparagus

Imperial/Metric		*American*
8 oz/225g	asparagus	1½ cups
	boiling salted water as needed	

- Cut off the tough bottom ends of the asparagus stalks, wash well, and scrape or peel off the white part.
- Tie in bundles and boil in plenty of salted water for 15 minutes or until tender.
- Drain well and serve with melted butter. Eat with your fingers as the first course of a meal.

Asparagus with peas combines the aphrodisiac effects of both foods; if you serve it in a sauce batarde (see recipe, page 107), you'll get the benefit of egg-yolk – much praised by Sheik Nefzawi – as well.

Asparagus and Peas in Sauce Batarde

Imperial/Metric		American
8 oz/225g	asparagus	1½ cups
8 oz/225g	shelled green peas	1⅓ cups
2 oz/55g	butter	¼ cup
½ oz/15g	cornflour/cornstarch	1 tbs
	salt and pepper	
	2 egg yolks, beaten	
	juice of ½ a lemon	

- Cook the asparagus in salted water till almost tender.
- Add the peas and continue cooking for a couple of minutes.
- While the asparagus is boiling, make the sauce:
- Take half of the butter and melt it gently in a saucepan that will hold over a pint.
- Remove from the heat and stir in the cornflour, working the mixture to a smooth paste.
- Pour 3/4 pt/425ml/2 cups boiling water steadily into the paste, beating the sauce well until smooth and free from lumps. The heat of the water should be sufficient to cook the cornflour.
- Allow the sauce to cool slightly, then add the seasonings and beaten egg-yolks. Keep the sauce warm but do not boil.
- Beat in the rest of the butter, a bit at a time in small pieces; stir in the lemon juice.
- Drain the asparagus and peas, and pour the sauce over them. Serve immediately.

The avocado, the final subject of this chapter, is not really a vegetable but a fruit. It has the qualities of both: specifically designed for eating, in the nature of fruit, but without the sweetness we would normally expect. In the place of sugar, avocados contain oils that give them the most seductively smooth texture.

The name avocado is derived from the Aztec word *ahuacatl*, which means testicle. I've never noticed any direct effect of avocado on the testicles, but the avocado does offer many benefits to our sex-lives.

One of the natural chemicals in avocado is *bromocriptine*, a drug that acts on those brain centres crucial for hormone regulation. Bromocriptine is prescribed for some forms of female infertility and hormone-dependent breast disease. In the high doses used medicinally, it can have unpleasant side-effects, but you suffer none of these when you get it naturally from the avocado.

Avocado is the most nutritious of the vegetables and fruits. It's chock-full of valuable vitamins, including C, E, B_6 and other B-group vitamins, minerals and essential fatty acids. So even if the bromocriptine content is too small to offer any significant benefit, the nutrient content is quite sufficient to justify the exalted position of the avocado in the good sex diet!

I like avocado in salads, its rich oily flesh cut into chunks, mixed with tomatoes and watercress, and coated with vinaigrette. Or you can mash it to create a dip to eat with your crudités, seasoned with cider vinegar, garlic and salt. Alternatively, just eat it on its own with vinaigrette. My recipe appears on page 109.

Vinaigrette

3 tbs organic cider vinegar
2 tbs cold-pressed extra virgin olive oil
½ tsp runny honey
¼ tsp fine sea salt
1 clove garlic, crushed

- Put all the ingredients in a screw-top jar.
- Shake well.
- It is now ready to pour into the hollow left by the removal of the stone from your avocado, or onto your salad.

Alternatively, women can use this vinaigrette (diluted with extra oil or water to reduce stinging) to soothe vaginal soreness.

Yes, I am serious. This is what I use in emergencies. Vinegar, garlic, honey and olive oil all have fungicidal and bacteriocidal properties, and they will reduce discomfort and itching. What's more, they complement your natural juices excellently – your lover might be surprised at the flavour of vulva vinaigrette, but he's not likely to object!

—10—
Light

My Fire

*L*ike many of the best aphrodisiacs, spices were banned by Puritans. They were said to 'provoke unseemly passion'. But the good sex diet isn't for puritans; passion is exactly what we want to provoke, and if dour individuals find it unseemly, I feel sorry for them – they don't know what they're missing!

Many spices can heat the senses. Ginger, cinnamon and nutmeg, cayenne pepper, saffron and cardamom; all are recommended. 'Kissing comfits', much enjoyed from Elizabethan to Victorian times, were made with honey and spices – usually ginger and nutmeg; and similar mixtures are described in *The Perfumed Garden* as remedies for a variety of sexual problems.

Nutmeg has a particularly strong reputation as an aphrodisiac, especially in China and the Yemen. Twentieth-century scientists have isolated a hallucinogen (a substance capable of inducing hallucinations) from nutmeg, which was popular for a while as a psychedelic drug in the late 1960s. However, if you take enough to get intoxicated – and that means about two whole nutmegs – you will make yourself unpleasantly ill; your hallucinations will be accompanied by headache and nausea, and the hangover will be profound and long-lasting. Definitely not recommended!

Smaller doses of nutmeg have less dramatic but more enjoyable effects. It is often the case that drugs which in high doses can produce intense changes in the mind, just heighten sensation and pleasure when taken in small quantities. Nutmeg is said to be of particular benefit to men who want to delay ejaculation; however, I cannot give a personal report on this property because it's not a problem I've met for some years, and none of my male friends admit to being premature ejaculators! Feedback from anyone who wishes to experiment would be appreciated.

You can use nutmeg in a great many ways: in cakes and biscuits, in egg custards, and with cooked vegetables such as spinach and mashed potato. If you want to use a lot, spiced cakes are the best option; the strong taste of nutmeg can easily overpower the flavour of eggs and vegetables unless you're cautious.

Simnel cake (see recipe, page 112) is an English spiced cake that was traditionally eaten on Mothering Sunday. Was this because all the spices in the cake fired up the couples who ate it to create more babies? In March, when simnel cakes were traditionally baked, the sap rises in the trees, the birds are courting noisily, and signs of joyful new life are everywhere.

Yet March nights are still long and cold, and we cuddle together for warmth – or at least, our grandparents did! Central heating may have reduced the physical need for close contact, and contraception has partially broken the link between sex and mothering, but Spring still gets most people's juices flowing with anticipation. It's the time of new awakening – so celebrate with a passion-provoking spiced cake!

Sexy Simnel Cake

Imperial/Metric		American
6 oz/170g	self-raising/self-rising flour	1½ cups
	pinch of salt	
	1 tsp grated nutmeg	
	½ tsp ground ginger	
	1 tsp ground cinnamon	
	1 tsp ground mixed spice	
	3 eggs	
6 oz/170g	brown sugar	1 cup
8 oz/225g	mixed dried fruit	1½ cups
6 oz/170g	butter	¾ cup
4 oz/115g	apricot jam/jelly	⅓ cup

This cake will serve eight people but it'll keep well. It's prepared in two layers and sandwiched with almond marzipan (see recipe, page 113).

- Pre-heat the oven to warm – 325°F/170°C (Gas Mark 3).
- Line two 8-inch sandwich tins (low-sided cake tins) with oiled greaseproof paper.
- Sift together the flour, salt and spices. Beat the butter and sugar together till smooth, pale and creamy. Beat in the eggs and fold in the flour and fruit.
- Divide the batter equally between the two tins and cook for 45 minutes.
- Cool in the tins for 10 minutes, then turn onto a wire rack.
- Spread the tops and sides with apricot jam.

Marzipan

Imperial/Metric		American
1 lb/455g	ground almonds	4 cups
1 lb/455g	icing/confectioner's sugar, sifted	4⅓ cups
	1 tbs lemon juice	
	½ tsp vanilla essence/extract	
	½ tsp almond essence/extract	
	a few drops of red food colouring	
	1 egg-white, beaten	
	2 egg-yolks	

- Blend the almonds and icing sugar together. Beat the egg yolks and add to the mixture.
- Stir in the lemon juice, vanilla and almond essences to make a stiff paste.
- Divide the paste into two. Lightly roll out each piece on a surface dusted with icing sugar.
- Cut out one 8-inch circle from each piece; top each half of your simnel cake (see recipe, page 112) with the marzipan, then place one on the other to form a sandwich.
- Work a few drops of red food colouring (or red mixed with a darker shade) into the remaining marzipan to create a flesh tint. Shape the marzipan into two entwined figures (or heart shapes if you're not that confident about your prowess as a sculptor!); arrange these on the cake.
- Heat the oven to very hot – 450°F/230°C (Gas Mark 8). Put the cake on a baking sheet and glaze the top with egg white. Bake for 5 minutes.

Ginger is a spice that's recently been recognized by Western medicine as having valuable therapeutic effects. It's a highly effective antidote for nausea, especially travel sickness. Eastern cultures have known this for a long time, of course; and they know a lot more about it besides. Ginger is said to add strength to a man's erection; he can either eat it or rub it (or have it rubbed) into his penis.

'A man with a small member,' the Sheik Nefzawi tells us, 'who wants to make it grand or notify it for the coitus, must rub it before copulation with tepid water, until it gets red and extended by the blood flowing into it, in consequence of the heat; he must then anoint it with a mixture of honey and ginger, rubbing it in sedulously. Then let him join the woman; he will procure for her such pleasure that she objects to him getting off her again.'

Preserved ginger is more suitable for this recipe than the dried, ground spice, which does not dissolve in honey; a gritty member is not to be recommended! Our method is to chew lumps of crystallized or preserved ginger until our saliva is well spiced; then we transfer the heat from our mouths to each other's sexual organs directly through licking, sucking, and titillation with our tongues. Ginger spices up '69' – mutual oral sex – in the most exciting way! You'll feel localized heating and enhanced sensitivity, without any soreness or discomfort.

We have proved the Sheik Nefzawi right time and again. The man's organ, well spiced with ginger, grows larger and more powerful; his lover shares his excitement in the most gratifying way. He does indeed procure the most tremendous pleasure for his partner – and for himself too. Discovering the delights of ginger is something for which we give heartfelt thanks to the publisher who encouraged me to research and write this book.

Those couples who would prefer the man to be a little better endowed should keep a pot of ginger by the bedside alongside their massage oils. It 'gingers up' one's sex-life like nothing else. There are no adverse effects; ginger is entirely beneficial.

Ginger is a mild stimulant which you can enjoy in many different ways. What about eating gingerbread to fortify you between bouts?

There's no need to restrict yourself to gingerbread men – unless, of course, it's only men you're interested in! So take a tip from the Greek and Roman prostitutes who used to make male and female couples of bread or cake to enact their fantasies, and create spicy gingerbread lovers to enjoy at your leisure (see recipe below).

Gingerbread Lovers

Imperial/Metric		American
9 oz/255g	self-raising/self-rising flour	2¼ cups
8 oz/225g	soft dark sugar	1⅓ cups
	pinch of salt	
	1 tsp ground cinnamon	
	½ tsp nutmeg	
	3 tsp ground ginger	
4 oz/115g	sunflower margarine	½ cup
	1 egg	
	bits of cherries, currants/raisins, almonds, etc., as needed	

- Pre-heat the oven to warm – 325°F/170°C (Gas Mark 3).
- Sift the flour, sugar, salt and spices into a bowl.
- Rub in the margarine with your fingers until the mixture is like fine breadcrumbs.
- Beat the egg and mix with the dry ingredients to form a stiff dough.
- Cut out human figures (make them as realistic as you like, using bits of cherry, currants, or chips of almond for detail!) and place them on well-greased baking sheets.
- Bake for 15 to 20 minutes.

If you want to go all the way, you can wash down your gingerbread lovers with ginger tea, a stimulating drink that will make you glow (see recipe below).

Ginger Tea

ginger root (1 tsp per cup), grated or chopped fine
water
honey to taste

- Add ginger root to the water and bring to a boil.
- Cover and simmer for a couple of minutes.
- Remove from the heat and let brew for a further 5 minutes.
- Sweeten with a little honey.

Of the spices used in savoury dishes, hot red peppers are reputed to be the strongest aphrodisiacs. Reminiscent of the Caribbean, and available in variety and profusion from West Indian grocers, peppers are wonderful, but they must be treated with caution – they can be hotter than you ever imagined!

Martin, an old friend, told us this story by way of warning about the hazards of peppers: Some years ago, he was working as a consultant to a new horticultural enterprise where they grew hot red peppers. The peppers were picked by young women from the local villages.

One day, a colleague came to visit him. He lingered while being shown around, obviously enjoying watching the women working. To spin out his time with the women, he showed great interest in the peppers, handling, picking and examining quite a lot of them. My friend, who realized that his interest was not really in the peppers, just let him get on with it. Curiously, the longer they stayed, the more interest the older women in particular seemed to show in their visitor.

Wherever they went, the women kept a careful eye on Martin's friend. Eventually, as they approached the office building, he went to use the men's room. When he emerged a short time later, red-faced and agitated by some unseen discomfort, he was greeted by hordes of giggling women waving the rubber gloves they wore for picking peppers.

So take care with hot red peppers! Limited heating of the sexual organs is wonderful, but you can be severely burned if you handle any delicate part of your body after touching them.

My gorgeous friend Charleen comes from Trinidad; the warmth of her island birthplace seems to suffuse her whole being, so that she brings a special glow to her adopted Welsh home. In Trinidad, the use of aphrodisiac spices such as nutmeg, ginger and hot pepper is a normal part of everyday life.

If my experience of men from Trinidad is typical, it must be a very sexy place indeed; I wonder how much the spices the natives enjoy in their food and drink contribute to the ambience? My Trinidadian lovers brought relaxed hedonism into my life like a warm breeze, blowing away the blues after a depressing series of relationships with guilt-ridden Europeans.

Charleen always wears surgical gloves to chop the small, fiery peppers for the sauce her mother taught her to make. These peppers can burn your hands; part-tamed and eaten in sauce (see recipe, page 118), they heat your whole body, from the inside.

Trinidad Pepper Sauce

Imperial/Metric		American
	1 dozen hot West Indian peppers	
	(or 18 chilli peppers)	
	2 cloves garlic, crushed	
	4 large onions, chopped fine	
¾ pt/425ml	vinegar	2 cups
	1 tbs sugar	
	1 tbs salt	
	1 tbs ground ginger	
	1 tsp curry powder	
	1 tsp turmeric	
	1 small courgette/zucchini (optional) chopped	
	2 tbs oil	
	1 tbs mustard	

Ideally, you should use small red West Indian peppers, which are much hotter than chillies, for this recipe. If you use chilli peppers, you'll need more.

- Wearing surgical gloves, chop peppers fine. Mix in the garlic and the onions.
- Bring the vinegar to the boil, add the sugar, salt, spices and mustard.
- Pour onto the chillies, onions and courgette, stir and bottle.

This sauce is wonderful with chicken fricassee (see recipe, page 119) – but do be careful not to burn your mouth by eating too much at a time!

Chicken Fricassee

Marinade:
1 large onion, chopped
3 cloves garlic
½ tsp salt
3 to 4 tbs vinegar or lemon juice
½ tsp thyme
2 tbs chopped parsley
2 tbs soy sauce
dash Worcestershire sauce
2 tsp pepper sauce (see recipe, page 118)
chopped spring onions/scallions or chives (to taste)
1 whole chicken or chicken pieces
Chicken Fricassee:
5 tbs sunflower oil
1 tbs sugar
salt and pepper to taste
water as needed
2 tbs cornflour/cornstarch
1 tbs cold water or as needed

- First, you'll need to make the marinade. Mix all the ingredients together and place the chicken pieces in it.
- Leave the chicken in the marinade overnight if possible. The longer you steep the chicken in it, the better the flavour will be. When you're ready to start cooking, remove the chicken portions from the marinade and set them aside to dry.
- Heat the oil in a heavy pot, add sugar, and let it burn. Yes – really!
- When it's black and smoking, add the chicken pieces, turning them quickly so they brown all over.
- Fry for 6 to 8 minutes, stirring. Season with salt and pepper.

- Cover the pot and cook on a low heat, either in the oven – at 325°F/170°C (Gas Mark 3) – or on top of the stove over a low flame; in Trinidad they cook chicken fricassee on fires on the beach, or on barbecues outdoors.
- Add water if the chicken looks to be drying out.
- Mix cornflour with a little cold water, and add the mixture to the chicken juices to make a gravy.
- Serve with pepper sauce (see recipe, page 118), sweet potatoes and fried plantain (available from West Indian and specialist grocers).

Cool your lips after this sizzling meal with a luscious ripe mango, sprinkled with nutmeg, so that the hot sun of the West Indies suffuses your whole being through the flavours native to those beautiful islands.

—11—
Alcohol: The Great
Disinhibitor

*A*lcohol is one of the most popular aphrodisiacs in the Western world. It works by releasing inhibitions, making it easier for people who grow up in a culture that represses sexuality to tune in to their desires. But alcohol is double-edged: as Macduff says in Shakespeare's *Macbeth*, 'It provokes the desire, but it takes away the performance.' What Shakespeare doesn't mention here is that it can sometimes take away the desire, too.

Alcohol is a potent drug which acts on the central nervous system to reduce anxiety. It has sedative, anaesthetic, muscle-relaxing properties that can work for you if you're tense but against you if you're tired. Drink too much, and you'll feel too zonked to cope with active sex. You'll be too insensitive to please your partner, and men can suffer the notorious 'brewer's droop', becoming incapable of sustaining an erection.

In Western countries, most people imagine that alcohol is fairly harmless, despite the fact that it contributes to thousands of deaths every year. You have to be careful with alcohol, and treat it with respect. Restraint is essential if you want to be a good lover.

The effects of alcohol on sexuality have been researched fairly thoroughly by psychologists and physiologists. Some of their discoveries are quite surprising, others predictable. For example, non-drinkers and light drinkers are similar in terms of frequency of desire and participation in sexual activity. But heavy drinkers experience much less desire and little participation.

Men are more likely to suffer detrimental effects on their sex-lives than women, because there's no female equivalent of male impotence. More promiscuous women drink more than others, but that just means they change partners more often, not that they enjoy sex more with each partner. Chances are the opposite is true: if you're having a marvellous sexual relationship with one person, you don't swap to another so readily.

Drinking can be a way of coping with dissatisfaction, blunting the pain of unhappiness. It can reduce your nervousness and fears of sex – but sometimes with disastrous consequences which leave you only with regrets next morning. When you're drunk it doesn't matter so much who shares your bed, and you can get a nasty shock when you wake up. Even when you are happy with your choice of partner, he or she may not be eager to repeat the experience. It's a very poor start to any relationship.

If you need alcohol to break through your sexual inhibitions, you'd probably be better off working through your problems with a counsellor so that you can enjoy sex fully when you're sober. Breaking down inhibitions with drugs doesn't work at all in the long term, and brings little satisfaction even in the short term.

Those who use alcohol as an aphrodisiac will be careful not to get drunk; they'll restrict their intake to quantities that make them feel merry without perceptibly disrupting their sexual performance. But this can be a difficult judgment to make, especially since alcohol damages our ability to make accurate judgments, whether in bed or on the road. People who have been drinking rarely recognize how severely they are incapacitated by it. They interpret stupidity as wit, clumsy pawing as exciting sex-play.

Research suggests that any alcohol at all can make men into poorer lovers; in one experiment, young men watched blue movies with their member wired up to strain-gauge transducers, which measure the penis' circumference. The results revealed that all doses of alcohol used inhibited sexual response.

So – alcohol shrinks a man's essential part! That's not an effect most people would want.

However . . . the size of a man's erection depends very much on his state of mind, and laboratory experiments don't measure the subtle effects of a couple of drinks taken in conducive circumstances. If alcohol in moderation makes you feel good, confident and relaxed, then the mental brakes on your sexuality will be dissolved and the strength of your erection will show the benefit. Laboratory science is far too cold a method to measure such effects.

Alcohol has another effect that seems to have been ignored by these laboratory researchers. It dilates the blood-vessels in the skin, causing flushing and a sensation of warmth. Flushing is part of your natural sexual response, while a warm skin makes you feel good, especially if the environment is just a little too chilly. So this aspect of the physiological reaction to alcohol could enhance your feeling of sexual arousal and pleasure.

Chronic alcoholism and frequent heavy drinking reduce desire through damage to sex hormone systems. Alcoholics often become impotent. The level of testosterone, the hormone that largely controls lust, is reduced by alcohol. Twelve hours after drinking six pints of beer, circulating testosterone falls significantly. This means that you're less likely to feel sexy the day after hitting the bottle – even if you aren't suffering from a hangover. So it's not just the short-term brewer's droop you should worry about: the effects last longer than most people realize.

Alcohol is just one of many drugs that depress the central nervous system and reduce sexual interest and responsiveness. Tranquillizers, sleeping pills, drugs for heart problems and high blood-pressure, and powerful pain-killers can have similar effects. Even nicotine interferes with sex. The sexiest people avoid regular or excessive use of drugs of all kinds, especially as many of these also interact with alcohol, making users more vulnerable to its damaging effects.

All that said, alcohol taken in small quantities is a social facilitator and a delightful taste experience. But always go for quality; be cautious about quantity.

If you're having wine with your sexy meal, stick to one bottle at most between you; and don't have any other alcoholic drinks. If you start with an aperitif, go on to wines, and finish the meal with spirits, you have had too much to expect the most exciting erotic experiences later. And while plying your partner with drink might decrease his or her resistance to your advances, you won't create the right circumstances for a night of exquisite sexual passion.

So beware the booze: it may seem to promise delights, but unless you enjoy semi-comatose incompetence, it can let you down. Use alcohol with care; disinhibition can lead to disappointment.

Using alcohol in food can be the best way to enjoy its effects without overdoing the quantities. Some of the recipes in this book include a little alcohol (see pages 57, 71, 76, 79, 83 and 125); enough to delight the senses but not so much that your pleasure will be reduced.

Zabaglione (see recipe, page 125) is a very special alcohol-based dessert which combines the properties of wine with the strengthening power of egg-yolks. However, if you make zabaglione, bear in mind the warnings about uncooked eggs (page 56), and be careful about the source of your eggs.

Zabaglione

Imperial/Metric		American
	4 egg-yolks	
	2 tbs caster/superfine sugar	
2 fl oz/60 ml	Marsala	¼ cup
	For serving:	
	4 *langue de chat*/long sweet crisp biscuits	

Marsala is a sweet wine, not dissimilar to sherry. To make the authentic version of zabaglione, you do need Marsala; but if you want to cheat, get some sweet sherry or fruit wine.

- Whisk the egg-yolks with the sugar in a bowl over a pan of hot water, until the mixture is pale and creamy.
- Slowly bring the water in the pan to simmering heat and gradually beat in the Marsala. Continue whisking until the mixture is thick and foamy. This is a recipe that requires patience and a strong arm; do not try to hurry it by turning up the heat, or your zabaglione will curdle.
- Serve warm in wine glasses with *langue de chat* biscuits.

Champagne

Champagne. It's the essence of celebration, the fun drink; *the* drink for newlyweds and lovers, for winners, film stars and millionaires.

The cork pops, a robust announcement of delights to come. Pleasure starts now! Cold bubbles tickle your nostrils, tingle on the taste buds, dissolving inhibitions so that laughter comes readily.

Truly, there's nothing like champagne!

Champagne is romantic, sexy, luxurious. Just imagine a champagne breakfast in bed . . . my friend Caroline says it's the greatest aphrodisiac of all. Champagne is the classic wine to have with caviar, oysters, all the most exotic aphrodisiac foods.

What more can I add? Well, champagne lovers must remember that no alcoholic drink is completely beneficial to your sex-life.

I am no wine expert; I can't tell you which champagne is the best or how to choose it – I just love drinking it! The real thing, of course, comes from the Champagne district of France, but there are many excellent sparkling wines produced by the *méthode Champenoise* that are also eminently drinkable.

So if you can't afford all the champagne you'd like, try tasting some of the lesser bubblies; there's much pleasure to be had with them.

Sparkling wines are more exciting because they are more stimulating, their impact more immediate than that of other wines. The carbon dioxide that bubbles through them increases the rate of absorption of alcohol by your blood-stream, so that the impact is more rapid. With non-fizzy drinks, blood alcohol and its mental effects rise more slowly, and you may have more than you want before you realize you've had enough. This danger is therefore reduced when you drink champagne.

But if you want the best boost for your sex-life, you mustn't have too much. One bottle between two people is quite sufficient. A couple of glasses of champagne can have aphrodisiac effects; a couple of bottles will reduce your ability to scale the heights of sexual pleasure.

So enjoy – but don't overdo it. Even with champagne, too much is too much. Enough, though, is wonderful!

—12—
Eating to
Stay Sexy

_N_ ow you know about aphrodisiacs, how the right erotic setting, good food, and a glass of your favourite drink can set the scene for a marvellously exciting time with your lover. You know about the exotic extras that can make your sex-life special, and about the basic principles of eating to maintain a high sexual drive. You know why micro-nutrients are important and why you need a good basic nutritional status to function properly.

This chapter will explain what this means on a day-to-day level, how to organize your diet so that it works for you.

Attention to everyday eating, as I explained in Chapter 3, is crucial. Many people neglect their real needs, eating from habit, choosing convenient food even if it's not the best thing for them. Some of us eat more than we need; most eat the wrong mix of foods.

Going on a diet has thoroughly unpleasant connotations. Most diets are depressingly unsatisfying; they fail to meet your body's needs, and however much you may want to believe in the promises that you'll feel wonderful, the reality is that you usually feel deprived. The good sex diet is not intended to make you hungry or to deprive you of the good things you need – far from it. In fact, feeling hungry – except for short periods before you eat – is counter-productive, both for good sex and getting slim.

If you stay hungry for more than a few days, you will start to train your body to store fat. Your metabolic rate will fall. That's not good for your energy levels or for your shape. So, on the good sex diet, you should not go hungry. If you are hungry, then eat! It's as simple as that.

Sometimes hunger creeps up unexpectedly, when we can't get a nutritious meal. People who skip breakfast and then find they're starving at 11 o'clock are very likely to go for sweets and chocolates; those who try to get by on coffee at lunchtime will face similar temptations by four. So think ahead; eat good nutritious food when you know your body needs it, so that you will be able to last the day without sugary snacks.

Breakfast, the first meal of the day, is often the worst. Do you habitually snatch a hurried bit of toast or a bowl of sugary cereal? That may not be what you need to build up your energy levels so that you can get the best out of the day. Give yourself sufficient time for a breakfast that will keep you going.

You may not want much food at breakfast time, but it is worth while ensuring that what you have is right. Porridge makes a very good start to the day because it releases its energy slowly, maintaining your blood-sugar – the source of immediate energy – at a constant level. Oats are rich in the best type of carbohydrate, absorbed slowly from the gut.

We enjoy porridge in the morning in the traditional Scots manner, without sugar or milk and with just a little salt for seasoning. If you choose the best organic porridge oats, you'll be delighted by their delicate flavour. I make my porridge special by adding a handful of mixed bran and wheatgerm to improve the texture and give it a nutty taste, mixing it simply with water. You probably know the recipe but I've given it in full on page 129.

Porridge

Imperial/Metric		American
2 pt/1.1lt	water	5 cups
8 oz/225g	oats	2 cups
	½ tsp salt	

ground almonds, wheatgerm, bran to taste

- Add the oats and salt to the water.
- Boil gently for 5 minutes, stirring all the while, until the mixture is thick and creamy.
- To make your porridge extra special, try adding a tablespoon of ground almonds to the mixture; this will enhance both its flavour and nutritional value.

Eating oats every morning will help your sex-life. According to the researchers of the Biodisiac Institute, oats have aphrodisiac properties. They are certainly very good for your whole body, especially the heart, because they can help reduce cholesterol levels. Oats are soothing to people who suffer from nervous tension, and they have special benefits for diabetics or anyone who's prone to blood-sugar fluctuations and hypoglycaemia.

If you really don't like porridge (and don't dismiss it if all you've tried are instant oats smothered with milk), then muesli (known as granola in the United States), made up of rolled oat flakes, fruit and nuts, is excellent too. I don't mean those sweet mixes produced by the multi-national food companies and supermarkets: muesli that contains added honey, sugar or other sweeteners does not have the benefits of those mixtures that contain only the natural sweetness of fruit and grain. I mean real muesli – organic if you can get it – which you can get from any good wholefood shop. Add some wheatgerm for extra nutrients, and eat it with a mixture of natural unsweetened yoghurt and skimmed milk.

For most people, a high-protein breakfast is unnecessary. Our bodies don't cope well with protein foods such as egg and bacon just after we've got up in the morning. But you may know from experience that you do better if you have an egg or a kipper first thing; we all vary. Experiment; tune in to your own needs, think about how energetic you actually feel after different kinds of meals.

Try to avoid tea or coffee with your breakfast. Herb tea or fruit juice will give you a better start to the day. I drink rosehip tea first thing in the morning; it's refreshing and gently cleansing. There are many delicious fruit tea mixes that you might enjoy too, or you may enjoy dandelion coffee, which is very good for the liver. Experiment with teas – don't just go for the ordinary kind: it's not so good for you, and it keeps you from getting the full benefit of the nutrients in your food.

If you like a mid-morning snack, try to avoid sweet biscuits. Eat if you're hungry, not otherwise, and choose an apple or wholemeal toast with a thin covering of sunflower spread or nut butter. If you're at work and you need something convenient, what about sugar-free oat cakes?

At lunch time, go for vegetables if you can. Very few people eat enough vegetables, and our health is the worse for it. A fresh salad, with tuna, beans, nut roast or an egg, will give you more energy for the afternoon than sandwiches or fried food. Baked potatoes with your favourite filling make a good alternative. But watch the butter or cheese content: fatty dairy products are not beneficial to your sex-life.

Some people like to eat their main meal at lunchtime; others prefer to eat more later. There are no firm rules about this; what suits you depends on your individual metabolism, your personal bio-rhythms. Just ensure that the food you eat is the most nutritious you can find at that time; always avoid processed and de-natured food.

If you prefer frequent snacks to considered meals, that can be fine so long as you choose your food carefully. Fresh fruit, nuts and seeds, natural yoghurt – all of these are convenient and quick to eat, yet full of goodness. A packet of raw nuts will be much better for you than crisps or a greasy hamburger; an apple or orange will do you far more good than a chocolate bar.

Bread – so long as it's whole grain, and preferably organic – is a good staple too, the best of the convenience foods. But do be careful not to smother it with butter, and choose your sandwich fillings wisely. Salad sandwiches are great, but not if they're running with fatty mayonnaise. Think about what you eat: it's crucial to the way you feel.

At dinner, the greatest part of your meal should again be composed of vegetables. Any vegetables – potatoes, greens, roots, peas, whatever you prefer. Vary your choice of vegetables from day to day, and go for fresh produce whenever you can. Raw vegetables – as crudités or in salads – are the best of all. Eat masses of salad made from the best fresh vegetables and fruits you can get. Watercress and spring onions are especially beneficial.

If you eat meat, beware of the fat content. Meat fat is not good for our bodies, especially when it comes from animals that have been reared under intensive conditions, exposed to a variety of chemicals and drugs. Pollutants concentrate in animal fat. It makes sense to cook meat so that the fat runs off, and to cut away excess fat.

Beware, also, of organ meats such as liver, kidney and heart. These concentrate pollutants, drug and hormone residues even more than does fat, so the nutrients they contain may be offset by the risks they pose. However, organ meats are very nutritious if they come from organically-reared animals. As the number of organic meat producers increases, you'll be able to get safe offal more easily.

From my research, I believe that we should avoid eating meat too often, or in large quantities. You're likely to be healthier if you eat meat just two or three times a week, not more. Stick to vegetable sources of protein, such as nuts, beans and tofu for most meals.

Fish is usually a better option for health than is meat, but tragically even fish is not as healthy as it used to be. With the pollution of the seas, fish – especially fish that live in shallow waters – are becoming contaminated with toxic chemicals. Tuna and pilchards are still safe because they come from seas that are relatively unpolluted. Farmed fish such as salmon carry dangers too: they are likely to contain residues of chemicals used to kill pests that thrive in crowded conditions. They also contain artificial colours from their feed; when fish such as salmon and trout don't have access to a natural diet, their flesh doesn't develop the pink colour that we want. So fish farmers add colour, just as poultry farmers add colouring to hen food to produce bright yellow egg-yolks.

Isn't it tragic that such wonderful foods as liver and fish are becoming health hazards? They should be a warning to us: we humans must clean up our act or suffer the consequences.

And suffer we do. The most sensitive organs to pollution in our bodies are our reproductive systems. The male testes, where sperm are produced, are very susceptible to chemical pollution. Sperm development and motility are damaged by low levels of a great many toxins. Not surprisingly, male fertility is decreasing in our increasingly polluted world. Even if you don't want to have babies, do you want to damage your body with chemicals that could make you incapable of reproducing?

It's primarily because of the pollution problem that I warn against full-fat dairy products. Here, too, chemicals are concentrated; for example, dairy produce is the main food source of dioxins, poisons so deadly that many experts believe there is no safe dose. If you eat a lot of full-fat milk, butter and cheese, you could be receiving dangerously high levels of dioxins. Pregnant women, in particular, should avoid full-fat dairy produce.

If your sexual activity is intended not just to give you pleasure, but to produce babies, it's imperative that you take special care to avoid toxic chemical residues in your food. Avoid fish from water that is likely to be contaminated by industrial pollution, such as the North Sea and rivers that run through industrial areas where toxic chemicals may be dumped. Avoid pork and bacon, which are fatty meats produced mainly in intensive farms that use a lot of pesticides and drugs.

Drink skimmed milk and eat low-fat cheeses such as Gouda, Edam and cottage cheese, or here in Britain cheese from relatively clean areas such as West Wales. Fortunately, there are increasing numbers of small cheese-makers in places that have few industries;

their products should be fairly safe.

Above all, eat low on the food chain, choosing vegetable products as much as possible, for they do not contain such high levels of pollution. This is why nuts and seeds, which are very nutritious and relatively free from chemicals, should form such important parts of our diet in today's disturbingly polluted world.

Nuts and seeds are very important for women, as I explained in Chapter 8. Not only do they contain the nutrients women need to maintain a healthy, sexy hormone balance, but they will help to protect you from the damage that could be done by chemicals. Raw sunflower seeds, Brazils and cashew nuts are particularly valuable. Eat them in meals, with salads, rice and grain dishes, or between meals as snacks to keep your energy levels high.

While the rule for everyday eating is to ensure that you are always well fed, over-eating of course will not help your figure or your sex-life. Some people can find it difficult to stop eating even when they know they've had enough, but do try to tune into your needs so you don't have more than you really want. However, you'll find it very difficult to eat vegetables to excess! You may eat so much you feel a bit bloated, but that effect will disappear quite quickly. So never worry about piling your plate high with vegetables – just so long as they aren't smothered with butter.

Eating plenty of vegetables, along with whole-grain foods such as organic rice, wholemeal bread, pasta and oats, will improve your figure and your general well-being. It will also keep your breath fresh and your whole body smelling and tasting wholesome. A diet that's high in meat, fat and animal protein will have the opposite effects. Those who've tried high-protein, low-carbohydrate diets will know how horrible they make them smell! So cut down on animal products and boost the fruit and vegetables – you will soon feel better for the change.

On special days, you can break all these rules. When you only have butter, cream, sugar, chocolate and all your favourite indulgences in a deliberately sexy meal, you'll not be taking the same risks as when you casually eat these things every day. And you won't feel as deprived and resentful as you would if you didn't ever allow yourself to have luxuries and wonderful gourmet food.

When you're planning an exciting evening, you can start acting according to a different set of rules. One rule that no longer applies concerns going hungry; when you're going to meet your lover you can fast for a while if you wish. If you're really excited, you'll lose your appetite anyway!

Fasting – not for very long, but for a few hours – will energize you when you know there's a treat in store. When you're slightly hungry, though basically well-nourished, your sex-drive may be enhanced. But you do have to know yourself well enough to know how much you can fast: if your blood-sugar levels tend to be unstable, you may have to keep nibbling. There's no sense in starting a night of indulgence irritable and headachy from lack of food!

A period of intense physical activity will have a similar effect to fasting; this is the best strategy for people who suffer ill-effects when they go without food for more than three hours. However, if you push yourself hard you may need a nap before you can tune into your heightened sexual drive. Activity depresses the appetite for a while, and you'll feel, look and smell your best a couple of hours after a physical work-out. So when you're planning to spend Saturday night seeing stars with your lover, try to devote the afternoon to fairly demanding activity. Or dance till you're feeling high with excitement, whether alone in your living-room, or on a dance-floor with your partner.

When you're ready to eat with your lover, all your appetites should be honed to a high pitch. You're bathed and perfumed, dressed up, sparkling with expectation. You're going to have a wonderful time. Don't let anything distract you from this simple aim; don't allow doubt into your mind; go all-out for pleasure!

For your sexy meal, keep the quantities fairly small. Go for quality rather than quantity. This is not the time to load your plates with vegetables, as you normally should. Large salads are marvellous for everyday eating, but a small and beautifully presented side-salad will make you feel sexier in the short term. Don't have too many potatoes, be cautious with bread and pasta, don't over-indulge with puddings.

Go for intense flavours, the best quality – but no excesses unless you're seeking the maximum wallop from chocolate! Savour your food. Now you're nourishing the mind; your body should already be well-nourished by your everyday healthy diet.

The reason for these words of caution is that large meals will make you feel sleepy. Carbohydrate, in particular, relaxes the body and mind, so if you eat a high-carbohydrate meal you could nod off shortly afterwards! Drinking alcohol will make you even more dozy.

Understanding the effects of different types of food on your mind and behaviour can be very useful when you want to achieve a particular effect. If you've been high with excitement and you want to sleep, use carbohydrate to re-balance your brain. Have a bowl of cereal, a baked potato, a piece of cake, or bread (no cheese!) to soothe your mind. Wash it down with a relaxing tea such as chamomile or Night-time. You'll find sleep will come more easily afterwards.

But when you want to be sexually active, you need food that has energizing properties. Eggyolk, as the Sheik Nefzawi knew, is one such food. So are chocolate and hot spices. Oysters and seafood can give you rapid-action energy too.

Carbohydrate foods such as potatoes, pasta and bread have a different type of energizing effect. Like a marathon runner, you can use a big carbohydrate meal on one day to give you lots of stored energy the next. These are slow-acting energy foods, foods you can use to build up your energy stores in the long term. But they aren't the stuff of heady excitement.

So when you're hoping your meal will be a prelude to sexual delight, choose foods from the earlier chapters of this book: aphrodisiac foods that will nourish and supercharge you without calming you down.

Avoid eating strong-smelling foods such as garlic, raw onions or curries, which will leave your breath tainted for a day before your great encounter. These may be fine for most days, but not when you want to be at your most desirable. Their effects can linger in some people for as much as 24 hours, so take care!

Finally, watch the booze. Try to avoid drink completely on the day before you intend to have a memorable time with your lover, and drink with caution when you're together. Two drinks is about the maximum for thoughtful lovers; if you drain a bottle of champagne between you, be sure that's all you have. Drinking more won't mean you have more fun: it'll interfere with your capacity to enjoy yourself as much as you could.

Suggested Menus

I've put these menus together to create a good balance of nutrition, textures and flavours. Use the recipes in this book to mix and match your own menus to your personal taste.

Menu 1
STARTER
Raw carrot and celery sticks
MAIN COURSE
Coq au vin (page 83)
or
Chicken in Pepper Sauce (page 118)
Fresh peas or beans
Creamed potato or boiled rice
DESSERT
Zabaglione (page 125)

Menu 2
STARTER
Avocado Vinaigrette (page 109)
MAIN COURSE
Fried oysters
Potato croquettes
Side salad
DESSERT
Chocolate Mousse (page 57)

Menu 3

STARTER
Raw oysters
MAIN COURSE
Steak in Roquefort Sauce (page 79)
Baked potato
Boiled carrots and peas
DESSERT
Pear Marilyn (page 62)
or fresh peaches

Menu 4

STARTER
Asparagus in Béarnaise Sauce
MAIN COURSE
Pasta with Walnuts (page 96)
Side salad
DESSERT
Green/fresh figs with fresh double/heavy cream

—13—
A Sexy
Body

*D*o you really want to be as sexy as you possibly can? If so, you'll need to get your body into the best shape attainable. Eating right will make it possible to achieve that, but diet is not all there is to it. You should also work on getting physically fit through exercise. When you get fit, you develop your energy stores so that you can achieve high physical output effortlessly, without tiring, puffing excessively, or putting unaccustomed strain on your heart. In addition, you will get your hormones into the best balance for high sexual desire and potency.

Partners are likely to fancy you more if you're trim and lithe, free from rolls of excess fat, with curves where there should be curves. Of course we don't just want to be fancied for our bodies, but why not make the most of what you have? You'll feel happier, healthier and randier.

What women find most attractive about men are firm buttocks and a slim waist; what most men like best are women who retain the firmness of their youth, without sagging or bulging where they shouldn't. For both sexes, the crucial factor is the *quality* of their flesh; not necessarily the quantity, for we are all born different shapes and sizes, and that diversity appeals to a diversity of personal tastes.

A quality body, for a person of any age, is strong, supple and lithe. That depends crucially on the condition of your muscles, and while eating the right food will help you to get into peak condition, it isn't the whole story. Activity is important too.

Few people are sufficiently active in their everyday lives to maintain anything near a state of peak fitness. We have to make conscious efforts to build regular exercise into our daily routines to compensate for the hours we spend sitting at desks or standing behind counters or on production lines; we have to balance our lives, compensating for inactivity with periods of deliberate action.

For exercise to work for you, it must be the right sort of exercise; but most important, it must be fun. If it's not fun you won't continue with it on a regular basis; and if you don't do it regularly, it won't offer the benefits you want.

Exercise is the key to being slim and fit for life. Diet alone will not burn off excess flab; if you restrict your food intake, all that happens is that your metabolic rate falls so that you need less food. People who go on slimming diets frequently get gradually fatter; 95 per cent of dieters are fatter a year after the diet than they were when they started! Dieting makes you fat: it's as simple as that.

Diet, in the sense of eating the right food, is of course essential. Unless we get enough of the nutrients we need, we won't have the energy for activity. And it's activity, and only activity, that burns up fat. Love-making helps, but it's not enough.

Exercise isn't merely good for you, it's also sexy. The moving body is inherently attractive: dancers and athletes command a huge audience because their lithe bodies in motion are tremendously desirable. To me, the sexiest image is that of a superb athlete running with a javelin; for Colin, it's female high-jumpers. Others admire tennis players or ice-skaters or divers. I'd rather watch my favourite athletes in motion than any blue movie! (Colin says he'd rather join his favourite athletes *in* a blue movie!)

It's not just the look of athletes that's so sexy. They *feel* sexy, too. In the past, before the threat of AIDS, I had many partners, and I discovered that athletes were particularly delightful. I've had the pleasure of making love to dedicated skiers, runners and martial arts enthusiasts; their muscle development was different, producing different bodily shapes depending on which sport they excelled at, but the qualities they shared were wonderfully firm flesh, well-proportioned bodies, and confidence in themselves as physical animals.

The activity that keeps bodies strong also gives them the energy for almost unlimited sexual pleasure. Whether your body type is slim, athletic, or tending to run to fat, you will benefit by getting your muscles as well-toned as you can.

It's a fact of physiology that the more energy you put out, the more you have available to use for pleasure; you develop your capacity to create energy. Surveys confirm this; regular exercisers report more sexual activity and more pleasure in it. The more you use your body, the more confidence you're likely to develop in your physical prowess, and the prouder you become of your body.

People who exercise more experience less depression and have more confidence. They are less prone to anxiety, hormonal problems, and many forms of illness, from diabetes to cancer. And, of course, they don't tend to suffer from weight problems. When you feel good about your body, it shows in your whole demeanour. You walk taller and your supple hips swing in a sexy way. You feel good wearing the most revealing clothes, and such self-confidence is attractive. When inactivity and poor diet make your body sluggish and sloppy, that shows too. Your skin will grow poor, pale and blotchy; your hair will be dull. Fewer people will fancy you. Don't let it happen!

So what sort of exercise do we need, and how much of it? This depends on your age and physical condition; young people can enjoy and benefit from strenuous exercise that would cripple their parents. But people of all ages look and feel better when they are regularly active. If you're getting on in years, regular exercise will help restore your youth, protecting you from all the forms of degeneration that afflict so many people in Western countries.

Everyone should aim to spend an hour, three times a week, in physical activity. For people under 30, this may mean strenuous games of tennis, demanding aerobics classes, running or other types of exercise that really get you sweating and panting. For those over 50 it's usually more sensible to spend that hour walking or cycling. But everyone's capacity for activity is different, and the more you do, the more you will be able to do.

The key is to work within your capacity and never try to break through pain barriers unless you are very fit indeed and know precisely what you're doing. Forget the 'no pain, no gain' myth: that might work for competitive athletes, but for those of us who just want to be fit enough to enjoy life to the full, pain is a warning signal that means we're overdoing it.

Overdoing exercise is counter-productive not only because it can lead to injuries, but because it puts you off continuing with your activity programme. What's the point in running till your legs are so sore you don't want to run again a couple of days later? Two or three less demanding periods of exercise will do you much more good than a single marathon.

So it's crucial to tune in to your own abilities and your own needs. Push yourself to the point where your body temperature rises and you're breathing hard, but not so much that you can't continue. A good rule is to do half of what you think you're capable of, and increase the amount gradually as you find out exactly what you can do without unpleasant after-effects.

In general, long-lasting, gentle exercise is better for shedding unwanted fat, especially when there's a lot of it to get rid of; the body's fat-burning systems don't switch on immediately, and if you exercise in short bursts – a quarter of an hour or less at a time – you cannot expect to use fat. For that length of time your body can work on short-term energy stores in the muscles, and you will experience little benefit. When you exercise for longer periods, you will train your body to burn off fat. Half an hour of continuous activity is the minimum you should aim for; an hour or more is better.

If you're already reasonably fit and you want to re-shape your body, building up attractive muscles or refining flabby areas, you will benefit from more demanding exercise regimes, such as weight-training and running. But the more demanding or strenuous the activity you take up, the more you need to make sure that you're properly equipped and that you know what you're doing. Joining a club, class or gym can be a good idea; the social contact adds to the fun, and trained instructors will be available to advise you.

Well-fitting, springy shoes are particularly important to protect your joints from damage. Go to a good sports shop and discuss your needs with an experienced assistant; don't just pick something up from the supermarket. Casual shoes might be fine for pottering about, but not for serious exercise; that requires specialized footwear.

Get the right clothes, too; clothes that don't restrict your breathing or movements. I prefer cotton because it absorbs sweat and breathes well. Put on plenty of layers so you can strip off as you warm up.

The best activity routines are those that combine different types of exercise. If you warm up with something that's not too demanding, such as cycling or brisk walking, then go on to strenuous activity, your body will gain more from it. Then, if you return to lighter activity, your muscles will use up the metabolic by-products of the demanding phase, protecting you from aches and discomfort later.

Demanding activity, which pushes up your heart rate and makes you breathe heavily, will increase your metabolic rate. This is very good news for people who feel they need only look at a cream cake to put on pounds; if they work their muscles enough to raise metabolic rate, they will be able to eat whatever they fancy – not all the time, but often enough to avoid feeling deprived – without suffering any ill-effects.

Any activity regime that puts demands on the muscles requires that your body is well-supplied with all the fuel and nutrients that your muscles need. That means eating whenever you feel hungry, and choosing wholesome food that will provide plenty of minerals and vitamins. If you don't eat properly, you won't enjoy exercise because you just won't have the energy. It doesn't make sense to deprive yourself of the nutrients you require; you will look and feel worse for it.

You may imagine that all this emphasis on exercise is just the current fashion, and that you don't really need to bother with building activity into your life to enjoy sex. That's nonsense. Exercise will make you feel sexier; this has been recognized for a long time. An ancient Indian text, the *Anaga Ranga*, says that women who have exhausted the body in sport or amusement will climax more easily. It's true, I can assure you!

The smell of a well-exercised body is more desirable, too. You continue to sweat for quite a while after a demanding activity session, and that fresh sweat contains pheromones that will excite your partner. My friend Inge likes nothing more than to jump on her Ian when he returns from a hard cycle ride, pink and glistening with sweat. She buys him sexy clothes for cycling: revealing, clinging shorts that define the shape of his muscular thighs and buttocks.

Some forms of exercise are inherently sexy. Dancing is the best example; it works your body and it's beautiful to watch. Salomé knew exactly what reaction she would get when she danced with her seven veils. Many of us are embarrassed to show ourselves off in this way, but what place does embarrassment have in our sex-lives? It can only do harm. Familiarity conquers embarrassment; the first time you dance for your lover you may feel silly, but the response you get should change your feelings completely. The second and subsequent times, you'll feel better and better.

Dancing with your lover can be an exciting form of foreplay as well as a marvellous emotional and physical release. Why don't we dance more, with more energy and abandon? We are far too prim and proper, too self-conscious, unwilling to let ourselves go and revel in our bodies. If we let ourselves go wild in the dance, that feeling will spill over to add to the excitement of the bedroom.

Another benefit of physical activity is the relaxation it induces. I've often set out on a run feeling tense, but the steady rhythm and muscular work drains all the tension from my shoulders so that I feel light and free after a mile or two. By the time I've come home and luxuriated in a hot shower, all the cares of the day have gone, leaving me glowing and receptive to the pleasures of the night.

Sometimes it can be difficult to summon up the energy to go out and run or go through a physical work-out after a demanding day. You feel tired, you'd rather flop in an armchair in front of the TV and forget about exercise. But the truth is that tiredness – which is death to sexual excitement – will often dissipate when you exercise. Tiredness often stems from a mental exhaustion that leaves you restless and irritable, worn out but unable to relax fully, let alone make love. Activity can re-balance your systems so that you can enjoy sex and sleep well afterwards.

It does take an effort of will. Exercise is not always easy to build into a busy schedule. But if you can make yourself do it, you will be glad.

I'm not going to recommend any specific exercise routine for improving your sex-life: any physical activity is likely to help. But there are two points you might like to consider. The first is the importance of a strong and supple back. All that hip-grinding makes demands on the lower back muscles, and the stronger they are the more varied the pleasures you can enjoy. To strengthen the back, whole-body work-outs such as the Canadian Air Force system described in the book *Physical Fitness* (Penguin, 1970) are particularly good. This graduated regime includes a variety of movements such as sit-ups and leg-raises in a balanced sequence that uses different groups of back and abdominal muscles, loosening and strengthening the spine and hip-joints.

Jane Fonda's workout as described in *Jane Fonda's Workout Book*, (Penguin, 1984) strengthens the whole body too. You might find it easier to work out with the video. But do take it gently; Ms Fonda has been practising for years! Of course she looks marvellous, doing that every day.

The second point is that the right exercise regime should strengthen your heart and improve your circulatory system. To gain these benefits, you should select activities that use your largest muscles, especially those in the legs. Exercise until you sweat and pant and your heart-rate goes up, and maintain this state of heightened energy output for 20 minutes or more. But you must do it three times a week; the improvements in heart function dissipate quickly when you stop bothering to exercise.

Sex makes quite heavy demands on the heart, especially for men. If you let your heart get out of condition, you may find yourself having to take drugs such as anti-hypertensives and beta-blockers, which are very bad for your sex-life. Many men on these drugs become impotent. Avoid this depressing fate with a balanced mixture of aerobic activity – exercise that makes you breathe heavily for a long period – and relaxation.

Rest is the essential counterbalance to activity. It's especially important to rest if you feel you're coming down with an infection, even a cold; never go on an exercise spree when you're feeling at all unwell. Putting demands on your body at that time will reduce your resistance and make you sicker than you need be. Similarly, if you start to feel nauseated or ill, or if you suffer pain in your joints when you're exercising, take it easy. Try again in a couple of days, and don't expect too much of yourself.

Always aim for pleasure in activity. Now I know that it's not always pleasurable when you start to work muscles that are unaccustomed to demand; your legs are likely to get sore when you start running or riding after weeks, months or years of inactivity. But you'll quickly learn the difference between temporary muscle soreness and serious strain. The former will pass in a day or so; the latter is likely to persist, and you should do your best to avoid it.

Exercise should be fun. Pick activities that give you pleasure. Martyrdom in the cause of physical fitness is counter-productive because it puts you off. So if you have always hated running, you should probably choose swimming or a gym workout; if you used to enjoy badminton, return to it; if you love the freedom of hill-walking, head for the hills! Start doing what you like regularly, and you will continue doing it.

Building activity into everyday life, perhaps by cycling to work instead of driving, or walking to the shops rather than taking the bus, is one of the best ways to achieve lasting fitness. When exercise becomes part of your daily routine, you continue doing it without noticing the effort.

When you walk or cycle, don't dawdle. The faster you go, the more you benefit. Go briskly, determinedly. When you dance, try to express the feeling of the music with your whole body, throwing yourself into your dance. Feeble foot-shufflers don't get nearly as much out of it as enthusiastic movers.

Half-hearted activity isn't as good for you, and it isn't sexy. Sexiness is impassioned, lively, full of energy. The more you incorporate these feelings into your movement, the more they become part of your self-expression. You'll learn to tune in to your vitality so that it switches on automatically, giving you the energy that you might have envied in others.

If you act middle-aged, you'll feel middle-aged. Act young, strong, and healthy, and those feelings will grow. We have many choices about the way we feel, the way we look, the way we are; to develop our sex-appeal, we need to make conscious choices that enhance our sexual, animal nature.

Fortunately, our culture has largely junked the idea that women should be feeble, weak, passive creatures. That was part of the pattern of thinking that kept women in an inferior position; it went hand in hand with the idea that women didn't actually enjoy sex, and their role was to accept whatever their masters gave them. Women today are more assertive, more positive about their own needs and pleasures.

Even so, many women fail to ensure that their own needs are met, whether in the bedroom or outside of it. Many neglect their activity needs, either because they are too busy looking after their families or because they don't realize how good activity will make them feel. It can appear easier just to deny your needs than to go to the trouble of ensuring that you get what you want.

But just as the effort of communicating with your lover to ensure that the right things happen to turn you on is time well spent in the long term, so time spent in physical activity is tremendously rewarding. We don't get much out of life unless we aim for what we want and put in the necessary effort. There may be a difficult phase at the beginning but it soon passes. Afterwards, you'll be really glad you bothered.

So if you value your sex-life, get out there and move your body! Your body is what it's all about: make sure it's in good shape.

—14—
Getting it
Together

*S*ex is one of the great forces of nature. As we grow up and our sex drive develops, it can become overpowering. I recall the years when I was phallus-happy, looking at every man in sexual terms, always judging whether I wanted him as a sexual partner. Nothing seemed to matter as much as this, even though I would struggle to convince myself that my work had to come first. In truth, I couldn't work anyway when my mind was taken over by lustful thoughts, my imagination constantly filled with fantasies of this man or that.

The power of the drive diminishes with the years, but it's still there, built into our bodies and minds. Neglected, it's like a serpent ready to strike at the most inconvenient moments, to cause havoc in our lives and those of others towards whom our passions are directed. Satisfied, it helps to keep us whole and youthful, however old we may be.

When I was growing up, sex and love were assumed to be inextricably linked for women, while men, it was said, could enjoy sex without love. Like many others touched by the sexual revolution of the 1960s, I discovered that this wasn't true: I could experience lust and enjoy sex with strangers. In due course, I learnt that love outlasts the brief fire of lust, but can rekindle lust again and again, building the foundation of a lifetime partnership that brings great joy.

Love can be very strong, yet it remains vulnerable. Sexual love is susceptible to all the pressures of our lives; it affects and is affected by the state of our whole selves. We live in a society where there are constant pressures that can diminish our sexual responsiveness, undermining our ability to love fully. It can be difficult to maintain that integrated wholeness of body and mind which allows both love and lust to flourish.

In partnership, we share our whole selves. The more we can share, the stronger the partnership and the more resilient our love. But if any part of our self is suffering or repressed, it can be difficult to sustain love. Often the sex drive is the first aspect of the self where damage begins to show.

Loss of desire, according to *Relate* (formerly known as the Marriage Guidance Council), is now the most common sexual problem between couples. This book is intended to point you to ways of firing up desire and bringing you closer together. Up to this point I've tended to concentrate on physical issues – building up the body so that it functions at its best, building excitement so that you can get the greatest pleasure. But the physical body is only part of the whole, and we diminish sex if we imagine that it's no more than an instinctive response of a healthy body.

Maintaining a high level of sexual desire within a long-term partnership requires that we nurture every aspect of our relationship. Living together is growing together; over the years, we are constantly exploring, discovering more about ourselves and our partners. When you think you know your partner as well as anyone could possibly know another, you still find corners that you never guessed existed: aspects of yourself and of your lover that had never emerged before. But this is a process that depends on trust and openness, on communication free from the constraints of fear and anxiety, on understanding and tolerance of your own needs and those of the person you love.

We must always be open to listening, never shutting the doors of perception, never refusing to acknowledge realities that are important to the person we love. We have to be open to the possibility of pain and unhappiness, of conflict and problems, for only when difficulties come out into the open can we expect to resolve them. There's no point in harbouring grievances or suppressing emotions; they only emerge more painfully later, growing in the darkness of neglect.

We should seize opportunities to show our positive feelings, show we care, demonstrate affection and desire when they well up within us, and nurture the expression of feeling by our partner. Telling your partner that you care, showing him or her by gesture and by action, will build confidence within your relationship; equally, accepting and acknowledging the expression of love from your partner will help sustain the fires of love.

The key to good communication, at all times, is honesty. We cannot afford to deny what we really feel, because that confuses and complicates our relationships in a way that can become disastrous. But while you are being honest about one aspect of your feelings, remember that you can also be honest about other aspects which may seem to exist in total opposition to it; we all have different mixtures of feelings, never wholly one thing nor another, the balance changing from time to time. So it's possible to temper any negative confrontation with warm and positive assurances that will keep you from breaking painfully apart while you deal with problems.

Life pressures unrelated to your relationship will affect the way you feel, the way you interact with your partner. Some may come from within yourself: they may be fluctuations in your hormone systems or other aspects of your physical function. Others will come from without; responsibilities at work, in the family, pressures in maintaining your home will all contribute their part. Sometimes you may fight because you're all screwed up about something quite unrelated to the apparent reason for your quarrel; sometimes your partner may attack you because of frustrations that are nothing to do with you. Don't immediately shy away, feeling personally rejected; keep your mind open to these pressures and tensions, recognizing that things may not be what they seem.

We have to be patient, generous and perceptive if we want to nurture our relationships. Fortunately, a loving relationship gives us access to patience and tolerance by building an inner strength and contentment that helps to sustain us through all the difficulties we may face.

If you have lost desire for your partner, or your partner isn't interested in sex with you, consider the pressures that may be acting on you both. It may not be a personal rejection; it might be that there just isn't enough energy to cope with everything at this time. Love and undemanding support may be the best therapy. Consider taking a holiday, if that's at all possible; and build more time into your schedule for yourselves, time when you can gently work on solving the problems that could be undermining sex drive.

Frequently, loss of interest in sex with a partner is the first sign of unresolved conflict within the relationship. Try to explore the feelings within and between yourselves; look for the turn-off switch that may be operating. Can you find a way around it?

Sometimes we turn off because sex has become boring or aversive. Communication and exploration of the problem can be the answer here. The worst thing you can do is ignore your lack of feeling and go through with sex for fear of your partner's reaction if you say no; that makes the situation worse. Tolerating sex when you don't want it creates resentment and bitterness, eventually destroying the love you once had. That way lies total turn-off.

But don't just say no and leave it at that for too long; abstinence unquestioned can become a habit that will detract from your lives and your relationship. Eventually one or both of you will seek other partners, with all the trouble that can bring.

Maybe in the long term you will part; maybe yours isn't really the right partnership. Maybe you married too young or on the rebound from a previous love and you've diverged with maturity. But giving up on a relationship should be the last recourse not the first one, even if your anger is flaring. There are always conflicts in relationships; there are bound to be compromises. A satisfying partnership is one that's capable of weathering crises and growing through learning from them.

Focus always on what you want to achieve. Build upon the strengths you find while investigating weak areas so that together you can find solutions that suit you both. Counselling is often helpful with this process; psychotherapy may help. I have been impressed by the power of psychosynthesis to aid in the process of discovering ways of dealing with issues that I had been unable to resolve on my own. But beware of seeking help from partisan friends or family who might have their own reasons for wanting to see you part, or who try to push you together without looking at the reasons why you're drifting apart.

Loss of sex drive can be due to health problems. If so, the good sex diet will help, along with sufficient physical activity and relaxation to keep you in balance. Even if you think that your difficulties are primarily emotional, work at the same time on building yourself up on the physical plane; this will keep you in a better mental balance.

Good sex depends on belief in yourself as a good lover. Learning about sex is helpful because you can't discover everything on your own; books such as Alex Comfort's classic *Joy of Sex* (Mitchell Beazley, 1986) may open your mind to sensual possibilities you hadn't dreamt of.

Some people feel that sex is only for the young, and that once they reach middle age, loss of interest is natural and inevitable. That isn't so; if you keep your body fit and your mind open, sex can be fun till you're a hundred. It won't be as frequent, but it can be more satisfying than ever before. Dismiss the images of the dirty old man or woman; they are pleasure-killing constructs of a society that doesn't value sex as much as it should. Humans can remain capable of enjoying sex and giving sexual joy to their partners until they die.

As we get older, we need more time for sex. Both men and women need more foreplay to get the juices flowing freely. Foreplay starts in the imagination, with thinking about sex and your partner as a sexual being; that's where the celebratory meals and lascivious treats described in this book can help you, however long you've been together. Erotica can stimulate you both; seek out books or videos that turn you on, and use them together to increase your mutual excitement.

Use the aphrodisiacs I've described for that extra fillip of excitement; enhance your passion with ginger, or chocolate, or whatever you enjoy most. I promise they work – my partner and I have tested them all! Researching this book has been very good for our sex-life. After 16 years together, and a period early on when we were actively studying sex, we didn't think it still held so many surprises for us. We have been proved delightfully wrong.

When you've been together for many years, using aphrodisiac foods, drinks and techniques can make sex more fulfilling than ever before. Tell your partner what's in store when you do this; knowledge of your actions and their implications will enhance the anticipation of pleasure for you both, and that anticipation will add to your delight. Long-term lovers will know what they both enjoy (though you will always discover more); you've lost that early self-consciousness and inhibition; you can communicate more freely. So use those advantages to the full. Don't let sex get boring or routine.

Massage can be a great boon, and new techniques are well worth learning. It enhances relaxation and focuses the mind on sensuality; it soothes tired muscles and eases mental tension. Buy oils perfumed with your favourite scents. We choose different massages for different times and different tensions; sometimes it'll be a foot massage, or a back massage; at other times we'll have a delicate face massage using moisturizing cream stroked gently into the skin.

There's one special massage I'd like to share with you. This comes from China, and it's called *The Serpent Rises*. It's a massage specifically for men; it enhances a man's sexual potency and the strength and size of his erection. This massage can produce the most incredible climax when you use it during foreplay; it doesn't speed up the response, but it makes it much more intense for both partners.

With the man lying on his belly, and his partner astride his legs, the masseur should first warm the oil in her or his hands. Stroke and caress the lower back, using firm movements on stiff muscles to relax them. Then, with your fingertips, trace the top edge of the hip-bone till you find the point where it meets the projecting part of the spine. You'll find a circular depression there, between the bones. Using your fingertips (or your knuckles if your nails are long), massage deeply at this point. The effects grow slowly, but they are dramatic when they develop.

Aphrodisiac treats, erotica, dance, massage, extended foreplay – all these delights that contribute to the growth and intensity of sexual excitement take time. Don't busy yourself with work till the last minute, flopping into bed exhausted. You won't have the energy then to get the most out of your sex-life. When the idea of sex appeals to you, make it a priority; ignore duties and the myriad day-to-day tasks. Retire early to give yourself all the time you need together.

The puritan work-ethic of our society can make it difficult for couples to give enough time to one another. Family commitments, lack of privacy and embarrassment about sex make it even more difficult. But sex is such a fundamental and important drive, one which can have such positive or destructive impacts on our lives, that we are foolish to stuff it into some dark corner of our minds, ignoring it when we construct our daily routines.

Sex is part of our natural heritage as living beings. It is an essentially individual thing that seems out of place in our institutionalized society. Our working lives put pressure on our sex lives, stealing the energy that should be available for pleasure. The state of the world damages our capacity to live fully, polluting our bodies, poisoning our reproductive systems. Sexual pleasure becomes elusive and distorted in overcrowded cities, overstressed communities, a society where frustration and discontent flourish as human values get trampled under too many feet.

Liberating our individual sexuality, experiencing our sexual power, helps keep us in tune with Nature. The capacity for great joy is built into each of us: let it flourish and enrich your life!

Recipe
Index

Other exciting titles from Thorsons:

Secrets About Men

Every Woman Should Know

Barbara de Angelis

If you have ever wished that men came with instruction booklets, you need despair no longer. Barbara De Angelis' best-selling *Secrets About Men Every Woman Should Know* is the book you've been waiting for since your first date!

Revealed in this book:

- Secrets about men and sex that men will never tell you
- The six biggest mistakes women make with men
- What men say . . . and what they really mean
- Men's top twenty turnoffs
- The five biggest mysteries about men
- How to spot — and avoid — the men who will give you the most trouble
- How to get the man you love to open up
- Techniques for becoming a more powerful woman

Barbara De Angelis is America's foremost relationships expert. This book will give you the tools you need to create the relationships with men that you always dreamed were possible.

Men, Love
and Sex
Joseph Nowinski

- What drives male desire?
- How can it be restored once it has waned?
- Where does it fit into men's own ideas of love and intimacy?
- How can a man and woman overcome the effects of male sexual problems, and rebuild their relationship?

Myths about male sexuality deny the existence of such problems as low sexual desire, inability to relax during sex, difficulty in maintaining erection or reaching orgasm, and premature ejaculation. The embarrassment and taboo surrounding these issues force many men — and couples — to suffer in silence.

Highly respected psychologist and sex therapist Joseph Nowinski uses proven sex therapy techniques, made accessible through case histories and easy-to-follow programmes — including special sections on sexual communication, building intimacy, and the uses of fantasy — which will help women and heterosexual couples to gain a better understanding of the male view of intimacy, love and sexuality.

An invaluable tool for professional counsellors as well as couples seeking to enhance sexual desire, *Men, Love and Sex* is a unique guide to a better sex life.

Sexual
Power
Sandra Sedgbeer

Sexual power is the key to having and getting everything you want out of life, and here at last is the book which will give to men and women the means to discover and use their sexual power to get not only successful personal relationships, but better jobs, and increase their network of friends.

Sandra Sedgbeer looks at what makes the essence of this mysterious quality, sexual power; it is not just the preserve of the Hollywood film star, but something that we all encounter every day. *Sexual Power* examines how our appearance can affect other people's reaction to us, and what kind of personality we appear to be projecting.

Having discovered and developed your sexual power, you can take on the world in the way that you have always deserved to do, and you will at last have the world working for you!